PRESENTED TO

Mrs. Sheila Taylor

FROM

David James

DATE

2014- 2015 CC Year

Thank
You!

QUIET MOMENTS

for

BUSY DAYS

Encouraging Thoughts

for Women

BARBOUR

Published by Barbour Books, an imprint of Barbour Publishing, Inc., P.O. Box 719, Uhrichsville, Ohio 44683, www.barbourbooks.com

Cover and interior design: Kirk DouPonce, DogEared Design.

Our mission is to publish and distribute inspirational products offering exceptional value and biblical encouragement to the masses.

Member of the
Evangelical Christian
Publishers Association

Printed in China.

Introduction

Our minds produce as many as 50,000 thoughts each day. That seems like an amazing number! But what's even more amazing is that approximately 80 percent of those thoughts are negative. How is a woman to defend herself against this dark and destructive onslaught in an already shadow-filled world? By immersing herself in the healing and protective powers of the Word of God.

Collected here are some of the most uplifting Bible verses you'll ever read, as well as a short devotion to inspire your heart and mind during the quiet moments of your busy day. Read them in the morning to get your day started right. Or read them in the afternoon to give you a quick boost. Or read them at night before you go to sleep. Simply make a pledge to feed your soul with positive, inspiring thoughts, using this little book as a launching pad to a better outlook and *in*-look toward your life.

There's no better time to start than today. Just turn the page and see how God's Word can shed His light in your heart, soul, spirit, body, and mind. Now that's a positive!

THE CREATIVE ZONE

God created human beings; he created them godlike,
reflecting God's nature. He created them male and female.

GENESIS 1:27 MSG

Genesis 1 reveals God as the ultimate Creator. Because we were made in His image, we also love to create. It feeds something in us, deep down inside. When we are in that crafting mode, creating "new worlds," we lose all track of time. That's because we are doing what we were made to do—adding beauty to the world. Working with our hands and minds, we are all artists, whether we are creating meals, knitting sweaters, or arranging flowers. For all the beauty we mold and shape is an expression and a reflection of the ultimate Creator God, not only working His way through us, but also looking back at us—and liking what He sees.

GOD REMEMBERS

*But God remembered Noah and all the wild animals
and the livestock that were with him in the ark,
and he sent a wind over the earth, and the waters receded.*

GENESIS 8:1 NIV

In the midst of our troubles, we may sometimes get the feeling that God has forgotten about us. Exhausted from sleepless, stormy nights, muscles strained from trying to hold on to the sides of a violently rocking boat, we moan and groan, asking, "God, are You there?"

Yet we need not fret. God always knows exactly what's happening in our lives. We need only have faith that He is with us before, during, and after the storms, knowing He will not only rescue us from deep waters but also set us upon dry land as troublesome waters recede.

THE GOD OF POSSIBILITIES

*Is anything too hard or
too wonderful for the Lord?*

GENESIS 18:14 AMP

There is no use putting limits on a limitless God! He can do anything—and everything! God can give a childless couple, past the age of childbearing, a brand-new, natural-born son. He can make a dry path through the sea. He can make the sun stand still. He can turn sorrow into joy, water into wine, and death into life. So why keep yourself from believing the impossible? Look to God. He has no limits. And as a daughter of God, neither do you. Keep your dreams alive, knowing God is the God of possibilities. There is nothing too hard or too wonderful for Him.

An Outstretched Hand

Lot's wife looked back,
and she became a pillar of salt.

Genesis 19:26 niv

It's simple. When we keep looking back to what once was, we do one of two things: We turn into a pillar of salt, grounded where we stand. Or, we trip up because our eyes aren't on the path ahead of us but upon what we've left behind.

So the only really viable solution is for us to allow God and His angels to get a good grip on us and hurry us out of the past. With our hands in theirs and our eyes on the path ahead, we will quickly find ourselves in a better place. All it takes is a willing heart, an outstretched hand, and faith in the One who is wiser than us.

FORMULA FOR SUCCESS

O Lord, God of my master Abraham, I pray You,
cause me to meet with good success today,
and show kindness to my master Abraham.

GENESIS 24:12 AMP

Before sending his servant to seek a bride for his son Isaac, Abraham told his servant, "The Lord, in Whose presence I walk [habitually], will send His Angel with you and prosper your way" (verse 40 AMP). In so saying, Abraham planted in his servant a seed of truth, faith, and optimism from the outset. Later, the servant prayed his own prayer in Genesis 24:12. When this prayer was answered, as foretold and believed, the servant immediately "bowed down. . .and worshiped the Lord" (verse 26 AMP). This is a wonderful formula for any of God's servants to follow: Envision success, pray for success, and then worship when success is obtained.

It's All Good

Joseph said to them, "Do not be afraid, for am I in the place of God? But as for you, you meant evil against me; but God meant it for good, in order to bring it about as it is this day, to save many people alive."

GENESIS 50:19–20 NKJV

Sometimes the unexpected happens: We are betrayed by loved ones, falsely accused by strangers, and discarded by society. The good thing about it is that no matter what happens to us, God means it for good. So there's no need to fret, seek revenge, or bad-mouth those who have hurt us. Instead, just continue hanging with the Lord. Have faith that He—the King on the throne and the one and only judge—knows what He's doing. And it's all good.

A HARD PLACE

Moses told the people, Fear not; stand still (firm, confident, undismayed) and see the salvation of the Lord which He will work for you today. For the Egyptians you have seen today you shall never see again. The Lord will fight for you, and you shall hold your peace and remain at rest.

EXODUS 14:13–14 AMP

Just when you feel trapped between the proverbial rock and a hard place, turn to God. He will find a way out you never dreamed or imagined. All you need to do is stand firm. The troubles that have come upon you today you will never see again in quite the same way. So, rest easy, no matter what is happening in your life. God will part any sea that you need to get through.

GOD'S PERSPECTIVE

What a great visual. Imagine God as a great eagle, carrying you out of all of your doubts, worries, fears. On His wings, you rise above all the pettiness, pressure, and pains of this world. He swiftly brings you into His presence. There, safe, warm, and secure, nothing matters but you and God. You look back down on earth and suddenly see all things through God's perspective. The mountains of obstacles you'd encountered on earth seem very small from this heavenly height. With a new perspective you return, knowing what once seemed impossible to scale is actually an effortless climb.

God's Already Been

"See, I am sending an angel before you to protect you on your journey and lead you safely to the place I have prepared for you. Pay close attention to him, and obey his instructions."

Exodus 23:20–21 nlt

Wherever you're headed, God's already been. He's got everything all set up. The beds are made, the fridge stocked. Your favorite book is next to a cushy chair, and your own special music is playing in the background. And God's already sent His angel ahead of you to lead and protect you on your journey. All you need to do is get there. Are you paying close attention to God and His angel, obeying His instructions, walking where He wants you to step? Remember: With God, obedience is the only surefire way to travel.

YOUR PERSONAL GOD

*"I'll set up my residence in your neighborhood;
I won't avoid or shun you; I'll stroll through your streets.
I'll be your God; you'll be my people. I am GOD,
your personal God who rescued you."*

LEVITICUS 26:11–12 MSG

Could you imagine God moving in next door to you and walking down your street, jazzed to be so near to the one whom He has rescued? Sounds amazing, right? But the fact is, God's already with you every minute of every day. He resides not just in your neighborhood but actually within *you*—and within all others He has rescued! All the power of His love, encouragement, and forgiveness is already inside of you. It doesn't get any more personal and empowering than that.

WELL ABLE

Then Caleb quieted the people before Moses and said, "Let us go up at once and take possession, for we are well able to overcome it."

NUMBERS 13:30 NKJV

Sometimes we cower in fear of the obstacles before us. Our imaginations take hold, making mountains out of molehills, monsters out of shadows. But then we remember God. We call to mind the idea that nothing can defeat Him. With God on our side, nothing can stand before us—no mountains, monsters, lions, leviathans, or Goliaths. We, like a courageous Caleb, can quiet our thoughts by saying—and believing—"I will go up at once and take possession of this situation, for I am well able to conquer it." Such words will transport us out of the shadowlands and into the sun of the Promised Land.

It's All in How You Look at It

*And Moses made a serpent of bronze and put it on a pole,
and if a serpent had bitten any man, when he looked to
the serpent of bronze [attentively, expectantly,
with a steady and absorbing gaze], he lived.*

NUMBERS 21:9 AMP

God wants our full attention on Him. Not just a quick glance, hoping He really doesn't notice us. Nor does He want us fearing that, when He does detect us, He may ask us to do something that, on the surface, seems impossible. With God, we are to have no fear. He wants our eyes on Him, "attentively, expectantly, with a steady and absorbing gaze." For that is the only firm focus on God that will truly save. So, today, do an about-face. Eyes front. Allow an eager focus on Your Father to banish all your fears.

GOD'S PROMISES

"God is not a man, that He should lie, nor a son of man,
that He should repent; has He said, and will He not do it?
Or has He spoken, and will He not make it good?"

NUMBERS 23:19 NASB

God's Word is chock full of promises for every believer. Since God does not lie, each and every one of those promises will hold true. Not just yesterday. Not just today—but tomorrow and all the days after that. What God has spoken, He will make come to pass. So shore up your faith by claiming each and every one of His assurances, knowing there is no limit to the promise fulfillment of a limitless God. What He did for Sarah, Hannah, Rahab, Naomi, Deborah, Abigail, Elizabeth, Mary, Lois, Eunice, and Dorcas, He will do for you—and so much more.

YOUR ENTIRE BEING

❧ ⚬🌀⚬ ☙

And now, Israel, what does the Lord your God require of you
but [reverently] to fear the Lord your God, [that is] to walk in
all His ways, and to love Him, and to serve the Lord your God
with all your [mind and] heart and with your entire being.

DEUTERONOMY 10:12 AMP

Your entire being." That's what God wants. No half-way devotion. No mere lip service. But you—heart, mind, body, soul—every ounce of you walking in His ways, loving Him, and serving Him. That means spending good quality time in His presence. Really listening for His voice. And then actually obeying Him, going where He wants you to go. Wouldn't you want your own child to do the same?

REAL TRUTH

It is the Lord Who goes before you; He will [march] with you;
He will not fail you or let you go or forsake you; [let there be no
cowardice or flinching, but] fear not, neither become broken
[in spirit—depressed, dismayed, and unnerved with alarm].

DEUTERONOMY 31: 8 AMP

It is easy to get distracted by the news. In fact, the words "depressed, dismayed, and unnerved with alarm" pretty well describe someone who has just watched the eleven o'clock newscast. But here's the thing—God's Word can wipe out all those emotions. A dive into Psalms can calm that palpitating heart. Some wisdom from Proverbs can soothe your nerves. How do you spell *relief*? GOD'S WORD. The real truth to live by—an anchor for the soul! Now that's deep!

Strength for Today

"As your days, so shall your strength be. There is no one like the God of Jeshurun, who rides the heavens to help you. . . . The eternal God is your refuge, and underneath are the everlasting arms."

Deuteronomy 33:25–27 nkjv

No matter what you have to do today, relax. God will give you the strength to do it! He will ride to your side to help you. He always has been, is now, and always will be around to help you. He will not only protect you but also fight for you. Just allow God's strength and power to work its magic. He's got you covered—today and tomorrow. So no matter how the situation looks, God is with you, upholding you, and giving you the strength to face whatever may come.

MAKE YOUR WAY

This Book of the Law shall not depart out of your mouth,
but you shall meditate on it day and night, that you may
observe and do according to all that is written in it.
For then you shall make your way prosperous,
and then you shall deal wisely and have good success.

JOSHUA 1:8 AMP

Because so many things in this society are vying for our attention, we can end up getting far off track. One way to keep ourselves spiritually fit and focused is to meditate, optimally daily, on God's Word. Find a Bible verse that nourishes your spirit. Write it out, and then speak it onto your heart. Allow its words and meaning to take root in you. Fulfill it in your life. Then, and only then, will you have prosperity, wisdom, and success. That's a promise.

Never Alone

"Have I not commanded you? Be strong and of good courage; do not be afraid, nor be dismayed, for the LORD your God is with you wherever you go."
JOSHUA 1:9 NKJV

In the first chapter of Joshua, God tells Joshua to be strong and courageous. He says this a total of four times! Apparently God was trying to get a very important point across: Because He is with us wherever we go, we *must* be strong and brave! And that's an order! So take heart, woman of strength and courage. You are never flying solo, no matter how detached from the rest of the world you may sometimes feel. Your pilot and navigator God is with you—whenever and wherever you go. No parachute needed.

THE GREATEST ROLE

*Now Deborah, a prophetess, the wife of
Lapidoth, was judging Israel at that time.*

JUDGES 4:4 NKJV

Women assume many different roles at different stages of their lives. We go from being daughters to students to graduates to career women to wives to mothers to grandmothers, and so on. With all those individual roles come many different hats, enough to sometimes drive you crazy. It's nice to know that back in the "old days," Deborah also assumed many different roles, including the "mother in Israel" (Judges 5:7 AMP). Yet the most supreme role she and we will *ever* play is that of being a daughter of God, the Most High King. Focusing on that role will give us the greatest wisdom and satisfaction in life.

Mighty Heroine

The angel of the LORD appeared to him and said,
"Mighty hero, the LORD is with you!"

JUDGES 6:12 NLT

When God went to see Gideon, He called him a "mighty hero"—and this was before Gideon had done any kind of fighting or rescuing. In fact, in verse 15, Gideon asks God how he, Gideon, will be able to save Israel since his clan is the poorest in his neighborhood and he is the least in his own father's house! Amazingly enough, God saw something heroic in him that Gideon had yet to reveal. So take heart. You, woman of strength, courage, and valor, are more than meets *your* eye! Grab hold of that truth and the added knowledge that *with God*, you can be and do anything!

A Fork in the Road

Ruth replied. . . "Wherever you go, I will go;
wherever you live, I will live. Your people will
be my people, and your God will be my God."
RUTH 1:16 NLT

Both Orpah and Ruth began to follow their mother-in-law, Naomi, as she started her journey back to Israel. But only one stuck with her to the end—Ruth. How many times do you turn around after Christ has led you to a fork in the road? Ask yourself: "Am I willing to go wherever Jesus takes me, to live where He lives? Are His people my people, His God my God, His Father my Father?"

Need to make a decision. . .choose a direction? No problem. Gather up all your belongings and head down the road with Jesus. Choose to stick with Him—no matter what—and you'll always find yourself on the right path.

A WOMAN OF STRENGTH

*And now, my daughter, fear not. I will do for you all
you require, for all my people in the city know that you
are a woman of strength (worth, bravery, capability).*

RUTH 3:11 AMP

It takes lots of strength to leave all you are familiar with
and go to a strange place, somewhere way out of your
comfort zone, to stick your neck out in an effort to pro-
vide for yourself and others. Yet when you do move out
with unshakable commitment and faith, people notice
your bravery, your capability. Even better than that, God
rewards you for your efforts. So simply have courage as you
continually seek His protection, and stay unwaveringly
close to Him as His blessings unfold for you—for you,
too, are a woman of His strength.

ALL AGLOW

*Hannah was speaking in her heart; only her
lips moved but her voice was not heard.*

1 SAMUEL 1:13 AMP

A tearful, childless Hannah poured out her heart to
God, asking for a son. When the priest Eli noticed
her, he thought she was drunk. After she corrected this
false impression, he prayed that God would answer her
prayer. Then she walked away, "her face radiant" (1 Samuel
1:18 MSG).

Although God can read your mind, He still wants to
hear what you have to say. Take some time to consider
the desire God has planted in your life. Then tell Him
all about it, knowing He is bound to fulfill your dream.
Afterward, as you rise from your knees, you, too, will
find yourself glowing.

Ears Wide Open

Then GOD came and stood before him exactly as before, calling out, "Samuel! Samuel!" Samuel answered, "Speak. I'm your servant, ready to listen."

1 SAMUEL 3:10 MSG

Could you imagine God standing in front of you, calling out your name? Would such a startling event leave you absolutely tongue-tied? Yet God is speaking to you each and every day. When you open up His Word or listen to a sermon, it's as if God is standing right there, calling your name! Are you paying attention? Listen up, ladies. God's looking for a few good women. Let Him know you're available. Tell Him, "Speak. I'm Your servant, ready to listen." When you're in tune with God, when your ears, arms, and heart open wide to His call, miracles abound.

WHAT REALLY COUNTS

GOD told Samuel, "Looks aren't everything. Don't be impressed with his looks and stature. I've already eliminated him. GOD judges persons differently than humans do. Men and women look at the face; GOD looks into the heart."
1 SAMUEL 16:7 MSG

Have you ever met someone who appeared to be beautiful—and then she spoke, her words marring whatever presentation she'd been trying to make? The old adage is true: beauty *is* only skin deep. So, it would behoove us to spend less time fighting physical fat and wrinkles and more time seeking God's spiritual form and face. With His presence developing deep within you, you'll find yourself shining with His light and reflecting His perfect love. That's a beautification process to die for!

OVER AND OVER AGAIN

The Lord Who delivered me out of the paw
of the lion and out of the paw of the bear,
He will deliver me out of the hand of this Philistine.

1 SAMUEL 17:37 AMP

God has saved you over and over again. First, helping you to rise above small challenges, then bigger ones. Thus there is no need to fear any new or bigger giants that may come your way. If God has saved you once, you can be confident He will be there for you again and again. And there's no need to arm yourself with a sling and some stones. You don't need them—for God is ready, willing, and able to not only deliver you but also fight the battle for you, over and over again.

NEVERTHELESS

❧

And the king and his men went to Jerusalem against the
Jebusites, the inhabitants of the land, who spoke to David,
saying, "You shall not come in here; but the blind and the
lame will repel you," thinking, "David cannot come in here."
Nevertheless David took the stronghold of Zion
(that is, the City of David).

2 SAMUEL 5:6–7 NKJV

David had a good habit of not listening to naysayers. His brothers and Saul told him that he, a boy shepherd, couldn't kill a giant. Now here were people telling David he couldn't take their city. "Nevertheless" he did! When you are faced with discouragers, giants, and strongholds, turn your back to them and grab hold of your own "nevertheless," knowing that with God all things are possible.

Your Shining Knight

*GOD is bedrock under my feet, the castle in which I live,
my rescuing knight. My God—the high crag where
I run for dear life, hiding behind the boulders,
safe in the granite hideout; my mountaintop refuge.*

2 SAMUEL 22:2–3 MSG

How wonderful to have a refuge in which to hide, a place where you know you are safe, where you will be looked after. God, like a knight, is here to save you from all harm, ready to sweep you up out of the swamp of trouble and carry you off! Although friends and family can bring you comfort, there's no need to run to them. Instead, it is better to run to the One whom no one can defeat—your shining knight, the almighty Lord, your all-powerful Father, the King, your Savior.

PROMISES SPOKEN AND FULFILLED

O Lord, the God of Israel, there is no God like You in heaven above or on earth beneath, keeping covenant and showing mercy and loving-kindness to Your servants who walk before You with all their heart. You have kept what You promised Your servant David my father. You also spoke with Your mouth and have fulfilled it with Your hand, as it is this day.

1 KINGS 8:23–24 AMP

When we wholeheartedly follow God, His words come true in our lives. He's not just talk. He actually moves mountains to keep His promises to us. When He speaks, it happens. Need a lift? Go to the Word and find a promise that speaks to your heart. Then believe it, and know that as You walk before your God, your eyes fixed on Him, that promise will become a reality.

TENDER CARE

The angel of the LORD came back a second time and touched him and said, "Get up and eat, for the journey is too much for you." So he got up and ate and drank.

1 KINGS 19:7–8 NIV

Elijah was on the run—literally. He was desperately trying to escape the evil Jezebel. Finally, exhausted and depressed, he stopped and sat under a tree, praying that he might die. What did God do? He didn't yell. He didn't lecture. He took care of His servant. He provided Elijah with food and rest. Once God renewed Elijah physically, He restored His servant mentally, emotionally, and spiritually until he could take up his mantle again, a stronger person than before.

Tired of running? Need a break? Go to God. Rest and restore yourself in Him. No one will care for you as tenderly as He.

SPIRITUAL FLIERS

*Suddenly a chariot and horses of fire came
between them [Elijah and Elisha]
and Elijah went up in a whirlwind to heaven.*

2 KINGS 2:11–12 MSG

Would that we could, at times, be beamed up by God—up and away from problems, challenges, and heartaches. Yet that's just what can happen, figuratively speaking. By lifting our hearts, souls, minds, and spirits up to God, we *can* rise above all the sorrows of this life. Whisked into His presence, we discover the kingdom of God within, and so obtain not only His compassion and courage but also His peace and perspective of this world. And the best part is that the more we rack up those spiritual frequent-flier miles, the more contented with all things we become.

OPEN EYES

"Don't be afraid. . . . Those who are with us are more than those who are with them." And Elisha prayed, "Open his eyes, LORD, so that he may see." Then the LORD opened the servant's eyes, and he looked and saw the hills full of horses and chariots of fire all around Elisha.

2 KINGS 6:16–17 NIV

When troubles and fears come our way, we sometimes have limited vision. We see only the physical and so our eyesight is limited to the standard 20/20. But if we pray and ask God to open our spiritual eyes as well, we will see His working in our lives, which may just include a multitude of horses and chariots of fire coming to our rescue.

COMMITTED CONFIDENCE

The field commander said to them, "Tell Hezekiah:
'This is what the great king, the king of Assyria, says:
On what are you basing this confidence of yours?'"

2 KINGS 18:19 NIV

No matter what, King Hezekiah clung to God. He never stopped following Him. Because of that, "the LORD was with him; he was successful in whatever he undertook" (verse 7 NIV). This gave Hezekiah the confidence to keep out the Assyrian army when it came knocking on the Jerusalem wall. After Hezekiah's passion-filled prayer, which ended with "LORD our God, deliver us from his hand, so that all the kingdoms of the earth may know that you alone, LORD, are God" (2 Kings 19:19 NIV), the angel of the Lord wiped out 185,000 of the enemy. Victory comes to the woman who doesn't cling to people or possessions but commits all to her confidence in God.

THE BIG BREAKTHROUGH

So [Israel] came up to Baal-perazim, and David smote [the Philistines] there. Then David said, God has broke my enemies by my hand, like the bursting forth of waters. Therefore they called the name of that place Baal-perazim [Lord of breaking through].

1 CHRONICLES 14:11 AMP

With its force and power, water can form grand canyons, sweep houses away, redefine a coastline. Yet God is even more powerful. Our God is a God of breakthroughs. With one swipe of His hand, He can upend our problems, give us peace amid chaos, break through barriers, bring down walls we, by ourselves, could never move. So never give up. Never surrender. Your "Lord of breaking through" is on His way, and your path will soon be clear!

An Active Faith

*Search for the LORD and for
his strength; continually seek him.*
1 Chronicles 16:11 NLT

What power those words from 1 Chronicles contain. How amazing it would be to live each moment of each day seeking and searching for God and His strength. What's even more amazing is that King David sang these words after the ark of God was brought into Jerusalem. Thus, even though the presence of God was within his walls, David still told his people to continually look for God. That's an active faith. A doing faith. A walking faith. Although God is within your heart, continually search for Him and His strength—around every corner, down every road, in every step. Seek God always—and in all ways—and you will be amazed at what you find.

On the Lookout

"You asked God for help and he gave you the victory. God is always on the alert, constantly on the lookout for people who are totally committed to him. You were foolish to go for human help when you could have had God's help. Now you're in trouble—one round of war after another."

2 Chronicles 16:9 msg

For one battle, King Asa asked God for help—and experienced victory. For the next fight, he went to a *human* king for help—and Asa lost. It's amazing how, even after God has worked major victories in our lives, we so often trust in people and things other than Him to help us, time and time again. For sure and consistent victories, lean on the solid Rock of Ages, not a permeable piece of shale. Remember, God's always looking for those totally dependent on Him.

RIVETED

We have no might to stand against this great company that is coming against us. We do not know what to do, but our eyes are upon You.
2 CHRONICLES 20:12 AMP

King Jehoshaphat knew a huge army was coming his way. At first, he was frightened, but then he "set himself [determinedly, as his vital need] to seek the Lord" (verse 3 AMP). In public prayer, Jehoshaphat bravely admitted to his people that he didn't know what to do. Yet that kind of public (or private) confession is just what God wants to hear. It's okay not knowing what to do. And it's even more okay to admit it. When we bow in humility and helplessness to God, He raises us up in strength and victory—because our eyes are riveted on Him.

A PROMPT TO PRAISE

You shall not need to fight in this battle; take your positions, stand still, and see the deliverance of the Lord [Who is] with you. . . . Fear not nor be dismayed. Tomorrow go out against them, for the Lord is with you.

2 CHRONICLES 20:17 AMP

Knowing God is with us and will fight our battles is a major relief! Why, with Him in our camp, there's no way we can lose! This kind of assurance, applied on a regular basis, will prevent stress, physical aches and pains, and depression. Just taking our positions and standing still—doing what we can and confidently leaving the rest up to God—is not only a wonderful remedy for what ails us but also an attitude that will prompt us to praise. And, just like Jehoshaphat's people, amid that praise, we will prosper and realize victory.

A Heart for God's Word

⁂

For Ezra had prepared and set his heart to
seek the Law of the Lord [to inquire for
it and of it, to require and yearn for it].

EZRA 7:10 AMP

Ezra was determined to eke out every last meaning of God's Word. To understand it and apply it to his life. Our study of God's Word should not feel like a chore. It should be something we crave. It should be as vital to us as the air we breathe, the water we drink, the food we eat. It should be our shelter, our clothing, our refuge. Ezra set his heart to seek God's Word and went on to lift a nation out of the abyss and back to God. Dedicated women of the Way can do the same.

STRONG HANDS FOR GREAT FEATS

They all wanted to frighten us, thinking,
Their hands will be so weak that the work will
not be done. But now strengthen my hands!
NEHEMIAH 6:9 AMP

Nehemiah refused to be frightened and discouraged when challenged with rebuilding and repairing the wall and gates of Jerusalem. Instead of listening to enemies and naysayers, Nehemiah prayed for God to strengthen his hands, to help him and the people do the work he knew God wanted them to do. The result? The wall was finished in just fifty-two days!

In order to accomplish a mighty feat, you, too, can pray with all your heart, "God, now strengthen my hands!" In so doing, you'll not only get naysayers out of your head but also astound them with your efforts.

Your Certain Place

*"Who knows but that you have come to
your royal position for such a time as this?"*

ESTHER 4:14 NIV

All who believe in Jesus are daughters of a King. Thus, if you believe, you are a royal princess! Pretty cool! But with that position comes some obligation. God has set you in a certain family, a place of employment, church, school group—any number of areas. And who knows but that you have been born at this time and in this place, in this royal position as a daughter of a King, to do something extraordinary for God.

Spend some time in prayer, asking God for what He would have you do. Then go forward and do it, knowing that God is with you every step of the way.

ULTIMATE ACCEPTANCE

His wife said to him. . . "Curse God and die."
JOB 2:9 NLT

We all have people in our lives who, when trouble comes, want to see us turn our backs on God and His Word. After all, doing so probably makes sense to them, so why not to us, right? Wrong. We know better. Just like Job, we can respond, "Should we accept only good things from the hand of God and never anything bad?" (verse 10 NLT). So, when times get tough, when it looks like all has been lost, when others are anxious for you to "curse God and die," keep your faith and keep your eyes on God, knowing that with and in Him alone is your hope and future.

THE POWER OF FOCUS

"What I always feared has happened to me.
What I dreaded has come true. I have no peace,
no quietness. I have no rest; only trouble comes."
JOB 3:25–26 NLT

What we focus on we give power to. If our minds, hearts, and souls are concentrating on the peace of Jesus, we shall have peace. Constantly worrying about "what ifs" will drive us from God's pathway. That's why the writers of the New Testament would have us think of good things, things that are lovely and praiseworthy. So, if you find your mind driving into the ditch, pick up your Bible and find some uplifting verses to get you back on God's highway. In so doing, you will discover His peace, revel in quietness, and luxuriate in rest.

A Midnight Mantra

In peace I will both lie down and sleep, for You, Lord,
alone make me dwell in safety and confident trust.
PSALM 4:8 AMP

If you ever have trouble sleeping, memorize the words to this verse and make it a midnight mantra. Commit to saying it in your mind at least ten times, and chances are, you'll fall asleep before hitting number six. Why? Because this is a truth that cannot be denied. In God, nothing can harm us. So there's no need to bother yourself with worries. No need to sleep with one eye (and both ears) open. Simply allow yourself to relax, imagining God is like the mattress that is supporting you, that holds you up. Close your eyes and go to sleep, knowing you can do so because God never does (see Psalm 121:4).

HOME SAFE

GOD's a safe-house for the battered, a sanctuary
during bad times. The moment you arrive,
you relax; you're never sorry you knocked.

PSALM 9:9–10 MSG

In this world, Jesus said, we'll encounter some trouble. But thank God for God! When we are being pursued, when we need shelter, when we feel as if we are running for our lives, we can go to Him. He will always be there for us—we merely need to remind ourselves of His presence. And, amazingly enough, as soon as we arrive on His doorstep, we know we are home safe. With Him, nothing can harm us. Back in His safe house, we breathe a sigh of relief, then find ourselves smiling, shaking our heads, wondering why in the world it took us so long to get ourselves there and asking ourselves why we left in the first place.

DIRECT ACCESS

In my distress [when seemingly closed in] I called upon the Lord and cried to my God; He heard my voice out of His temple (heavenly dwelling place), and my cry came before Him, into His [very] ears.

PSALM 18:6 AMP

Our Lord is so many things. Our Rock, Refuge, Shield, Deliverer, Strength, Hiding Place. . .The list goes on and on. No matter what our situation, no matter what our agony, no matter how hemmed in we feel on every side, we can call out to our Lord and He will hear us. There's no call waiting. We have direct access. And as soon as He hears our cry, He begins reaching out His arms to lift us out of the muddy pit or deep waters we've gotten ourselves into. Oh, what a Savior!

An Enlightened Way

You light a lamp for me. The LORD, my God,
lights up my darkness. In your strength I can
crush an army; with my God I can scale any wall.
PSALM 18:28–29 NLT

When we feel all is lost, we may, at first, turn somewhat reluctantly to the Word. After all, solely focused on our troubles, we barely have the energy to reach out for God's help and guidance. But we do so anyway because God's Spirit within compels us. The Holy Spirit knows that not only will the light of God's Word reveal our situation for what it truly is—temporary—but it will also give us the strength, strategy, power, and light to overcome any darkness.

No Lack

The Lord is my Shepherd [to feed, guide,
and shield me], I shall not lack.

PSALM 23:1 AMP

God gives us food, guidance, protection. He leads us to a place where we can refresh and restore our souls and spirits. We need not fear, for He has His rod to defend us and His staff to steer us. And if we, for some reason, should veer off the path, chances are He'll leave the other ninety-nine and come after us. What love and commitment!

Each day, take the time to envision following the Lord to lovely pastures. In His presence, lie down and listen to the trickle of a stream before you. Know that the Lord, your Shepherd, is all you need. Because of Him, you shall not lack.

God's Goodness

I would have lost heart, unless I had believed that I would see the goodness of the LORD in the land of the living. Wait on the LORD; be of good courage, and He shall strengthen your heart; wait, I say, on the LORD!

PSALM 27:13–14 NKJV

There are times when we are so low it's almost hard to breathe, so grieved that we cannot see beyond the shadows. It is then that we need to take the words of Psalm 27:13–14 to heart. Know, live, and breathe the fact that you *will* once again see God's goodness just where you stand, in this land of the living. He *will* lift you up, shine His light, reveal His wonders. It may not happen overnight— but it *will* happen! So take heart. Be brave. Wait for God to work His magic. For He undoubtedly will.

New Direction

You are my hiding place; you protect me from trouble.
You surround me with songs of victory. . . . The LORD says,
"I will guide you along the best pathway for your life.
I will advise you and watch over you."

PSALM 32:7–8 NLT

On those days when we feel we cannot face the world, we have a place to hide—in God. He is our refuge *and* our outer, impenetrable shield. He will build us up and, before we know it, we will be coming out from our hiding place, smiling and singing, knowing God has given us the victory. From that point forward, a new road map is made. He gives us new direction, showing us the best way to go, all the while keeping His eyes on us, making sure we come to no harm.

WORD POWER

The LORD merely spoke, and the heavens were created.
He breathed the word, and all the stars were born.

PSALM 33:6 NLT

What power our God has. He says just a few words, and the sky is born. He simply breathes, and all the stars and planets suddenly pop into existence. And the wonder of all this is that He is still speaking His Word into each person's life today. He is constantly creating new and breathtaking things. What's even more awesome is that we have access to His powerful, all-creating words. They can be found in the Bible. Today, speak one of God's promises into your life. Believe it is true. Then stand back and watch it manifest itself—another one of God's wonders before your very eyes.

SOLELY DIFFERENT

The LORD looks from heaven; he sees all the sons of men. . . .
He fashions their hearts individually.

PSALM 33:13, 15 NKJV

There are all kinds of unique people in this world, from the swirl on the top of their head to the footprints they leave behind. So it's no wonder we may chance across people who rub us the wrong way—and vice versa. Yet our Maker knows we are all different, each having a special talent to share or role to play. So if someone is getting on your nerves, stop and consider how, although different, we all are the same in one respect: We are here to love one another and God. Then praise Him for fashioning each of our hearts individually. And ask Him for the strength to respond to all with His love.

HEARTILY WHOLE

Our inner selves wait [earnestly] for the Lord;
He is our Help and our Shield. For in Him does
our heart rejoice, because we have trusted
(relied on and been confident) in His holy name.

PSALM 33:20–21 AMP

We all have a God-shaped hole in us, an inner yearning to connect with our Creator. And when, in prayer, we feel ourselves united with Him on a deep spiritual level, we cannot help but smile. For His presence cannot help but fill our hearts with joy and light.

Having trouble making that connection? Then do a heart check. Are you relying on Him—and only Him— for everything, with complete trust and total certainty? If not, surrender all to Him today, and then ask and allow Him to make you heartily whole.

ALREADY THERE

*God met me more than halfway, he freed me from
my anxious fears. . . . God's angel sets up a circle of
protection around us while we pray. . . . Young lions on
the prowl get hungry, but God-seekers are full of God.*

PSALM 34:4, 7, 10 MSG

When you can barely cry out because you are muted with fear, God rushes over. He is instantly by your side, unlocking the chains of anxiety and trepidation holding you captive. From the first word of your prayer to the last, His angels are clamoring in, protecting you on every side. Within that circle, nothing can touch, harm, or disturb you. Because you have sought God, He has taken up residence within you, filling you with His joy and presence. Lean back on God today. Imagine His angels surrounding you. Revel in the fullness of God-given freedom.

EVEN DEEPER

The LORD is near to the brokenhearted and saves those who are crushed in spirit. Many are the afflictions of the righteous, but the LORD delivers him out of them all.

PSALM 34:18–19 NASB

There is something comforting knowing that God is right there when your heart is aching or broken, when your spirit seems totally crushed—by the death of a loved one, a divorce, the loss of a very-much-needed job, or a terminal illness. When you are at your lowest, take solace in the fact that God is by your side, wiping away each of your tears with His gentle hand and drawing you even deeper into Himself and His embrace. Allow deep to call to deep, knowing you will yet praise Him.

DREAMS AND DESIRES

Delight yourself also in the Lord, and He will give you the desires and secret petitions of your heart. Commit your way to the Lord [roll and repose each care of your load on Him]; trust (lean on, rely on, and be confident) also in Him and He will bring it to pass.

PSALM 37:4–5 AMP

When you get yourself into God, finding the joy of being with Him more valuable than anything else in life, He can't help but make your secret heartfelt desires come true. As you commit all that you are to Him—putting each and every worry and fear onto His much stronger and broader shoulders, fully trusting He will make all come out right—He'll turn your dreams into reality—regardless of whether you are nine, forty-nine, or ninety-nine. You can depend upon it—and Him.

The Ultimate Support

The steps of a [good] man are directed and established by the Lord when He delights in his way [and He busies Himself with his every step]. Though he falls, he shall not be utterly cast down, for the Lord grasps his hand in support and upholds him.

PSALM 37:23–24 AMP

The bad news is we may go through some rough patches in this life. The good news is we won't be going through them alone—nor for very long. When we follow the path God lays out for us, we find Him on every corner. Delighted in our direction, He focuses on each step we take. And as soon as He sees us stumble, He reaches out, grabs our hand, and gets us back on our feet. Walking God's way, we have all the support we need to bear up under anything—and everything!

ALL IN ONE

He drew me up out of a horrible pit [a pit of tumult and of destruction], out of the miry clay (froth and slime), and set my feet upon a rock, steadying my steps and establishing my goings.
PSALM 40:2 AMP

Not only does God lift you up out of the deepest abyss, out of the ooze in which you'd almost sunk, He sets your feet high upon a rock to keep you secure and close to Him. He holds on to you until you are steady. He teaches you how to walk again and helps to put you back on the right path. All in one verse, God proves to be your rescuer, protector, and guide. It doesn't get much better than that!

GETTING AWAY

❦

Let be and be still, and know
(recognize and understand) that I am God.
PSALM 46:10 AMP

I t's time to stop running around. Get away from all the distractions, everything that is vying for your attention. Stop, stand, sit where you are. Simply be still. Don't just do something; stand there! Take three deep breaths and revel in the stillness that is part of God's perfect peace. To any issues that come up in your mind, respond with "So, what. . . . God is taking care of all." In other words, let all things be. In this stillness of body and mind, rest in, know of, and seek God's face. He's waiting. Allow your soul to fly away from the world and meet Him where He is, spirit to Spirit.

THAT SECRET PLACE

He who dwells in the secret place of the Most High shall remain stable and fixed under the shadow of the Almighty [Whose power no foe can withstand]. I will say of the Lord, He is my Refuge and my Fortress, my God; on Him I lean and rely, and in Him I [confidently] trust!

PSALM 91:1–2 AMP

Constantly living in communion with God, nothing can disturb your peace of mind. Steadily abiding with and in Him, there is a peace beyond understanding, for you know that God can vanquish anything and everything—fear, hatred, grief, sorrow. Such a life is a testimony to others of your living faith and the strength, protection, and power of your God. And it all begins in that secret place where you can "take refuge and be confident until calamities and destructive storms are passed" (Psalm 57:1 AMP).

ONE HEARTFELT VERSE

I will meditate on Your precepts, and contemplate
Your ways. I will delight myself in Your statutes;
I will not forget Your word.

PSALM 119:15–16 NKJV

It's one thing to read God's Word. It's another to meditate upon it, really taking time to soak in it, allowing it to cover you from head to toe with meaning and deliberation. Then to take the Lord's truth and memorize it, hiding it in your heart so that it becomes part of your life, ready and able to lift you, help you, shield you, free you, guide you. What's one heartfelt verse you can hide in your heart today, one that in all likelihood will save you tomorrow? Think about it. Revel in it. Memorize it. Own it. Live it. And stand amazed at God and His Word-power.

LOOKING FOR HELP

❦

GOD guards you from every evil, he guards your very life.
He guards you when you leave and when you return,
he guards you now, he guards you always.

PSALM 121:7–8 MSG

Where do you look for help and strength? To Mother Nature? To other people? To money? How about turning to the God who created everything, the One who breathed each of us into being. He will never let you stumble. He is awake while you sleep. He is your guardian, always at your side, keeping you safe—from things visible and invisible. It was true yesterday. It's true today. It will be true tomorrow. Need or want anything? Look to God. Seek His face. And, as you go out and as you come in, you will be safe, in heaven and on earth.

A SECOND OPINION

Search me, O God, and know my heart; test me and know my
anxious thoughts. Point out anything in me that offends you,
and lead me along the path of everlasting life.
PSALM 139:23–24 NLT

We think we know what our shortcomings are, the things we need to work on. But sometimes we need a second opinion. That's where God comes in. Only He, it seems, can reveal what is truly in our hearts and minds. After all, our holiness is an inside job—and God's just the person to do it. It is He who will help us discover what is not in line with Him and what we can do to change things up. Once we've received a good examination from the Great Physician, the right remedy is not far behind.

Mouth Guard

Set a guard, O LORD, over my mouth;
keep watch over the door of my lips.

PSALM 141:3 NKJV

How easily things seem to slip out of our mouths. In the heat of an argument, irretrievable words tumble out. In our distractedness, thoughtless phrases pass our lips and we are unaware of their effect on others. So what are you, a woman of the Way, to do? Ask God to place a holy sentry, a guard over your mouth—not so much to shield your teeth but to protect others from potentially painful criticism, cutting insults, and angry barbs. Instead of such discourse, take the right course: Go with compliments instead of criticism, insights instead of insults, blessings instead of barbs. Speak with love, and witness the healing power of your words.

WAKE-UP CALL

Cause me to hear Your loving-kindness in the morning, for on You do I lean and in You do I trust. Cause me to know the way wherein I should walk, for I lift up my inner self to You.
PSALM 143:8 AMP

What a joy to wake up in the morning, hearing the sound of God's adoring voice. What an awesome start to anyone's day. And how about returning the greeting by raising your arms to the heavens, exclaiming, "Good morning, God! What are we going to do today?" By exhibiting your trust in Him at the break of day, you'll be setting up the pattern for the hours to come, until night falls, and your heart, mind, body, and soul are again cradled in His arms.

THE RIGHT PATH

*Trust in the LORD with all your heart and do not lean
on your own understanding. In all your ways acknowledge
Him, and He will make your paths straight.*

PROVERBS 3:5–6 NASB

God is all-knowing, all-seeing, all-present. That's why you can trust Him to make the right decisions, to steer you in the right direction. It doesn't matter if what He wants you to do seems illogical or incomprehensible. God can see everything everywhere—past, present, and future. But we mere earthbound mortals have extremely limited vision. So trust that God will always know better than you, your friends, and your relatives. Put all your faith in Him, follow His directions, and you will always be on the right path—His.

HEART WISE

Guard your heart above all else,
for it determines the course of your life.
PROVERBS 4:23 NLT

King Solomon, a supposedly wise man, did not watch his heart very carefully. During his reign over Israel, he fell in love with many foreign women and ended up following their gods. In fact, 1 Kings 11:4 says that "his wives turned his heart after other gods; and his heart was not loyal to the LORD his God" (NKJV). As a result of his split loyalty, the country of Israel divided after his death. So heed diligently Proverbs 4:23. Keep a sharp eye on where your heart's desires may be leading you, and above all else, make sure it's not away from but toward God, the pilot of your life.

Exposé on Thoughts

For as he thinks in his heart, so is he.
PROVERBS 23:7 AMP

It's amazing how many things we won't put down the garbage disposal because we know what will clog, injure, or fatally wound it. Yet we are not, perhaps, so vigilant with what we put in our own heads. The phrase "You are what you eat" could equally apply to thoughts: "You are what you think." If you expose your mind to nothing but dire, discouraging, and destructive information, you're bound to be a negative person. If you expose your mind to hopeful, encouraging, and affirming information, you're going to be a positive person. So keep your mind on praiseworthy things. When you do, you'll be so much more apt to worship than worry. What do you think?

THE TRUTH OF GOD'S MATTER

The believer replied, "Every promise of God proves true;
he protects everyone who runs to him for help. So don't
second-guess him; he might take you to task and show up your lies."
PROVERBS 30:5–6 MSG

God's Word is truth. Every promise He makes will be upheld. Knowing He will never forsake us and never let us go is the mental armor we wear and spiritual weapon we bear as we go forth into this world. Along with this confidence, we must be content with what God has chosen to reveal to humankind in His Word. Thus, we are not to add to it, for He has already laid out in the Bible all we need to know. Endeavor only to rest and trust in God and the Word He has gifted us—both amazing treasures beyond compare.

A NATURALLY VIRTUOUS WOMAN

A good woman is hard to find,
and worth far more than diamonds.

PROVERBS 31:10 MSG

The woman described in Proverbs 31:10–31 is enough to make anyone wonder how she could ever become such a strong woman, or even come close! Yet it obviously can be done. How? By being a woman of strong faith and spirit. If a woman's heart, mind, body, and soul are dedicated to and worshipful of God, all the other virtues of Proverbs 31—willing to work, constructive, wise, gracious, generous, fearless, encouraging, financially prudent, dignified, watchful—will come naturally to her. Charm and beauty are nice but are not needed by a virtuous woman who spends more time reflecting upon God than her own image in the makeup mirror.

CHANGE

There is an appointed time for everything.
And there is a time for every event under heaven.

ECCLESIASTES 3:1 NASB

We go through many transitions in life. Some of those are brought about by God—the seasons, birth and death, sowing and reaping. Others are brought about by our own choices—crying and laughing, holding on and letting go, breaking down and building up. We witness the waxing and waning of things in our own bodies as we grow from girl into woman, and beyond. Instead of resisting these inevitable changes, those within and outside of our control, may we revel in the present and praise God for each transition that draws us closer and closer to Him, our Rock and our Refuge, the One who never changes.

THE POWER OF LOVE

Love is as strong as death, its jealousy as enduring as the grave. Love flashes like fire, the brightest kind of flame. Many waters cannot quench love, nor can rivers drown it.
SONG OF SOLOMON 8:6–7 NLT

Love is the greatest force in the universe, for love is God. And nothing—not even the greatest rivers and oceans—can separate us from or overpower that love. What an amazing force, our love for God and His love for us. It cannot even be overcome by death, as Christ proved when He rose again. And how wonderful to know that we have the power to extend this love not only to God but to each other. Who can you empower with your love today?

PERFECT PEACE

You will guard him and keep him in perfect and constant
peace whose mind [both its inclination and its character]
is stayed on You, because he commits himself to You,
leans on You, and hopes confidently in You.

ISAIAH 26:3 AMP

When your focus is on God and stays there, you will
experience heavenly peace. And not just peace
with and in God, but with other people, circumstances,
yourself, the past, and the future. This inward, outward,
backward, forward peace is what you find yourself tending
to seek more and more as you realize that nothing else in
this world but complete dependence, trust, and hope in
God can give you the serenity you long for. With God
guarding the door to your mind, how can you *not* have
peace?

ASKING FOR DIRECTIONS

❧❧❧

Your ears shall hear a word behind you, saying,
"This is the way, walk in it," whenever you turn
to the right hand or whenever you turn to the left.

ISAIAH 30:21 NKJV

Whenever we ask God for help, He immediately responds. The problem is that too often, instead of calling out to God, we try to make choices or decisions based on our own knowledge, experience, or hunches. Even worse is when we ask the advice of anyone and everyone *but* God! Yet God has told us that He is more than willing to direct us—and *He's* the One who truly knows what's best for us. So, have a decision to make? Stop. Ask God for guidance. Listen for His answer. And then, and only then, move forward.

SIMPLY REMEMBER

Have you not known? Have you not heard? The everlasting God, the LORD, the Creator of the ends of the earth, neither faints nor is weary. His understanding is unsearchable.

ISAIAH 40:28 NKJV

We *do* know and we *have* heard it before. But sometimes we apparently need a reminder that God is humongous, inexhaustible, wise beyond measure, constantly vigilant, and forever compassionate. There is nothing that will surprise Him. There is nothing we have done or will do that He won't forgive. Remember the infinite one? He sees everything and everyone. He's more powerful than any foe. And He's got your back. So relax. Simply remember: There is no one and no*thing* like our mighty God!

The Master

*He gives power to the weak, and to those
who have no might He increases strength.*

ISAIAH 40:29 NKJV

We want to be involved in lots of things—to help out at church, school, the community, and our own family. But when we do it all in our own energy, we're bound to run out of *oomph* at some point. So when you do find yourself weakening or completely out of strength, call on God. He'll power you right back up—and may even give you guidance as to what activities to continue and which ones to forgo for now. Because, although it's wonderful to be of service to others, your main obligation is hanging out with the Master.

LIKE EAGLES

But those who wait for the Lord [who expect, look for, and hope in Him] shall change and renew their strength and power; they shall lift their wings and mount up [close to God] as eagles [mount up to the sun]; they shall run and not be weary, they shall walk and not faint or become tired.

ISAIAH 40:31 AMP

It's awe-inspiring to watch eagles flying high above the earth. How they soar on those wings! It's such an elegant demonstration of their power and strength. We, who don't just tap our toes while waiting for the Lord, are like those eagles. We "expect, look for, and hope" in God, knowing that He will renew us, recharge us, the closer we get to Him. Keep this in mind as you take flight today.

Remember God

"Don't be afraid, for I am with you. Don't be discouraged, for I am your God. I will strengthen you and help you. I will hold you up with my victorious right hand."

ISAIAH 41:10 NLT

How awesome not to be afraid, to have our strength so tied up with God that we come out of nail-biting situations victorious! And that's what this verse promises us. So no matter what you might be up against, how scary a situation may seem, how dark the future looks, remember God. Remember who you are in Him. Consider how much He's done for you already. Take strength from His Word. And walk on, knowing that in Him you have all the victories you need.

DIRECT COURAGE

This is what the LORD says—he who created you,
Jacob, he who formed you, Israel: "Do not fear."
ISAIAH 43:1 NIV

I n His Word, God keeps telling us not to be afraid. In
fact, there are at least 365 do-not-be-afraid-type phrases
in the Bible—one for each day of the year. That must
mean God really wants us to get it through our heads,
know it in our hearts, declare it in our minds, and confirm
it in our souls. God, who intricately formed you, knows
exactly what you are afraid of. So wise up and listen up.
He's telling you directly not to let your particular fears
overcome you. How cool is that?

Lighten Up

"*I have called you by name; you are mine. When you go through deep waters, I will be with you. When you go through rivers of difficulty, you will not drown. When you walk through the fire of oppression, you will not be burned up; the flames will not consume you. For I am the LORD, your God.*"

ISAIAH 43:1–3 NLT

Each one of us wants to matter, to be known and loved by someone—someone who will never leave us, no matter how bad things get. And each of us has that "someone" in God. He has called you by name! He's known you forever! You are His royal daughter. No matter what happens—or where or when—He is with you. So lighten up! You never have been and never will be alone.

Change Up

*"Forget the former things; do not dwell on the past.
See, I am doing a new thing! Now it springs up;
do you not perceive it? I am making a way in
the wilderness and streams in the wasteland."*

Isaiah 43:18–19 NIV

God is constantly changing things up. But people who are stuck in the past or freaked out about the future can miss these new things coming up right now. Such women are letting the past and the future suck out the energy of and blur the vision of what He is creating today! So take a good look around you. Where is God working in your part of the world today? What new thing is He waiting for you to see and take up? Seek—and you'll find it. Move out—and He'll pave your way.

God's Baby Girl

*Even to your old age I am He, and even to hair
white with age will I carry you. I have made,
and I will bear; yes, I will carry and will save you.*

ISAIAH 46:4 AMP

Holding a precious baby is one of the most wonderful experiences you can have in this life. You find yourself simply marveling at her ten tiny toes and ten tiny fingers and awestruck at her look of complete dependence upon you. That must be how God feels when He carries you. No matter how old you are, you will always be His baby girl and, whether your hair is that of a newborn or an old woman, you will never be—and never have been—out of His arms.

FATHER KNOWS BEST

"I am the LORD your God, who teaches you what is best for you, who directs you in the way you should go. If only you had paid attention to my commands, your peace would have been like a river, your well-being like the waves of the sea."

ISAIAH 48:17–18 NIV

How many times have we made a decision without first consulting God and then ended up facing a lot of trouble and heartache? If we had not only listened but also obeyed His words, we would have been filled with immense peace and well-being. So the next time a decision comes up, go to God first. Pay attention to Him. Find direction in prayer and in His Word. Then, and only then, move forward in His way, confident that God the Father knows best.

THE MASTERMIND

Seek the LORD while you can find him. Call on him now while he is near. . . . "My thoughts are nothing like your thoughts," says the LORD. "And my ways are far beyond anything you could imagine."

ISAIAH 55:6, 8 NLT

Why do we want to seek God and call on Him? Because He is *the* mastermind. He is the ultimate in wisdom. He thinks of things we'd never dreamed or imagined, and hence, never even considered! With Him there are no limits! There is no box to think outside of! So, if you've got some choices to make, things to consider, run to God. Seek Him out. Call His name. Ask His advice. He'll blow your human mind!

FRUITFUL WORDS

"So is my word that goes out from my mouth: It will not return to me empty, but will accomplish what I desire and achieve the purpose for which I sent it."

ISAIAH 55:11 NIV

God's Word bears amazing fruit. Once it is tasted, it roots itself in our minds and cannot be shaken loose. It then begins to bear fruit in our own minds and lives. Anyone who reads or hears the Word is changed. All that the Word provides—promises, maxims, proverbs, enlightenment, predictions, guidance—achieves God's particular purpose. Where are you sowing the seed of God's Word today? Because of you and His Word, what fruit will God be harvesting tomorrow?

HOPE-FILLED PROMISE

"I'll show up and take care of you as I promised. . . . I know what I'm doing. I have it all planned out—plans to take care of you, not abandon you, plans to give you the future you hope for."

JEREMIAH 29:10–11 MSG

Some days things just don't seem to go right. We wonder if we're on the right track, doing what God created us to do. Or are we walking down a path He never wanted us on in the first place? Not to worry. If you are headed the wrong way, God will show up, cut you off at the pass, and turn you in the right direction. He knows what He's doing. He's got it all planned out for you. Your future is safe in His hands. That's His promise.

GOD'S PERSPECTIVE

"I am the LORD, the God of all the peoples of the world. Is anything too hard for me?"

The above verse is similar to what God said to Abraham and Sarah after she laughed at the idea of becoming pregnant in her old age (see Genesis 18:14). Two other times, God asked people if they thought His *arm* was too short to accomplish things (see Numbers 11:23 and Isaiah 59:1). But Jesus put a different twist on these verses, saying, "What is impossible for people is possible with God" (Luke 18:27 NLT). Looking at things from our limited perspective, we see impossibilities. But when seeing things from God's promised perspective, suddenly a myriad of solutions abound. Got a problem? Go get God. He's got the answers you need.

FONT OF KNOWLEDGE

Call to Me and I will answer you and show you great and mighty things, fenced in and hidden, which you do not know (do not distinguish and recognize, have knowledge of and understand).

JEREMIAH 33:3 AMP

It's humbling trying to imagine all the things we don't know. Fortunately, we have God, who knows it all. He sees things that have been hidden for eons. And He is thoroughly familiar with everything—in heaven and on earth, visible and invisible. But how do we access this far-reaching knowledge? Through prayer, meditation, and reading God's Word. Just pose God a question, ask for an answer, and keep your eyes and ears open. He'll show you what you need to know.

STUCK ON EACH OTHER

There's one other thing I remember, and remembering,
I keep a grip on hope: GOD's loyal love couldn't have
run out, his merciful love couldn't have dried up.
They're created new every morning. How great your
faithfulness! I'm sticking with GOD (I say it over and over).

LAMENTATIONS 3:21–24 MSG

O ur God is a God of abundance. His love and mercy for us have no end. They are newly made every morning. How wonderful, this endless supply of second, third, fourth, fifth chances for us. No matter how much we've messed things up by our words or acts, God will still love us and have mercy on us. He's so stuck on us, we can't help but be stuck on Him.

THE SEEKING WOMAN

GOD proves to be good to the man who passionately waits,
to the woman who diligently seeks. . . . When life is heavy
and hard to take, go off by yourself. Enter the silence.
Bow in prayer. Don't ask questions: Wait for hope to appear.
LAMENTATIONS 3:25, 28–29 MSG

What great advice for us on days when we are troubled and weary of life, with no energy left to nurture anyone—including ourselves. Go to God, your refuge, whether it be a physical place or a mental one. Walk into the silence and commune with the Master. Don't worry about what to say or ask. God knows what's on your mind. Just expect His answer and His presence, as promised to all women who diligently seek.

TRANSFORMED

"I'll give you a new heart, put a new spirit in you. I'll remove the stone heart from your body and replace it with a heart that's God-willed, not self-willed. I'll put my Spirit in you and make it possible for you to do what I tell you and live by my commands."
EZEKIEL 36:26–27 MSG

When you allow Jesus into your heart, everything changes. You become more gentle, more sensitive to others. You find your priorities, concerns, and dreams are different. It suddenly seems easier to understand God, and you begin thirsting for His Word. You are a new creature in Christ. With a brand-new heart and spirit, you are transformed, ready and anxious to make today and every day all about God, in whom you live, move, and have your being. Suddenly anything for God is possible. Remember that as you step into this day.

ALONGSIDE

"I see four men loose, walking in the midst of the fire; and they are not hurt, and the form of the fourth is like the Son of God."

DANIEL 3:25 NKJV

There are times in life when we feel as if we have been forced into a fiery furnace. With no apparent chance of escape, we cry out to God, "Where are You, Lord?" Yet we need not shout. For Jesus, the Son of God, is in that furnace with us. Whatever trial we face, we can be assured that He is walking alongside us. *And* that we will not only come out of this situation, but will do so intact. It's nothing but the best of God for those who trust and serve Him!

A PRAISEWORTHY LESSON

"When my sanity returned to me, so did my honor and glory and kingdom. . . . Now I, Nebuchadnezzar, praise and glorify and honor the King of heaven. All his acts are just and true, and he is able to humble the proud."

DANIEL 4:36–37 NLT

It's amazing what happens when we let pride come between us and God. When Nebuchadnezzar accredited all his greatness to himself and himself alone, God announced the great king would become beastlike—and he did! Then, when predicted, Nebuchadnezzar's sanity returned and he once again reigned, even greater than before in riches and humility, giving all credit to the Lord God. A praiseworthy lesson for us all.

ANGELS WON, LIONS ZERO

Then the king. . .commanded that Daniel should be taken up out of the den. So Daniel was taken up out of the den, and no hurt of any kind was found on him because he believed in (relied on, adhered to, and trusted in) his God.

DANIEL 6:23 AMP

King Darius passed a law stating no one was to pray to anyone but him. Daniel, knowing full well that this edict was in effect, prayed to his God anyway—and he did so "three times a day, just as he had always done" (Daniel 6:10 NLT)! Because of Daniel's courage and steadfast faith, he survived the lions' den with nary a scratch on him. So be bold and brave in faith today, knowing God's angels will disempower any lions you may face.

THE HOLY GRID

What are you waiting for? Return to your God!
Commit yourself in love, in justice! Wait for your God,
and don't give up on him—ever!

Hosea 12:6 MSG

How many times do we get sidetracked and begin doing things in our own strength, forgetting that God is the ultimate power source? Why do we always seem to wander away from the holy grid? It's time to stop being impatient, running ahead of God, and doing things on our own. Stop. Turn around. Head back to God. Commit to Him, allowing His love to flow through you. Be assured that all good things will come to you, a woman who waits patiently on the Master.

DREAMS AND VISIONS

*"I will pour out my Spirit on every kind of people:
Your sons will prophesy, also your daughters. Your old
men will dream, your young men will see visions. I'll even
pour out my Spirit on the servants, men and women both."*

JOEL 2:28–29 MSG

You are a servant of God and a believer in Christ. As such, the Holy Spirit hasn't just been sprinkled on you. He has been *poured out* on you! Your cup runneth over! As you continually obey God, the Spirit empowers you more and more. What dreams and visions is He giving you? Are you living them out? Ask God for clarity and guidance today. Know that you are the Spirit-filled dreamer God envisioned before you were even born.

Do-Gooders

Seek good and not evil—and live! You talk about GOD,
the God-of-the-Angel-Armies, being your best friend.
Well, live like it. . . . Hate evil and love good,
then work it out in the public square.

AMOS 5:14–15 MSG

To follow Christ is to continually seek to do good. Not just talk about it—but be so filled with love for God and His people, that we can't help but do the right thing! And not just in church on Sundays or on mission trips. But everywhere! Every place on this earth is a mission field for God, for doing the right thing, for being honest, selfless, loving, kind, decent. Humbly take responsibility when due. Remember that doing the good thing is doing the God thing.

The Boomerang Effect

As you have done, it shall be done to you;
your dealings will return upon your own head.

Obadiah 1:15 amp

There's no doubt about it. What we do will come right back at us. We will reap what we sow, some of it sooner rather than later. So what are you sowing? Seeds of love, respect, honor, humility, selflessness? If so, that's what you'll reap further down the road. So the next time you feel exasperated by fellow humans—the kids, your husband, the boss, your in-laws, your siblings, your parents, a complete stranger—take a deep breath before you say or do anything. Ask yourself, "Would I want this boomeranging back at me?" Then proceed accordingly.

Dry Land

*"When my soul fainted within me, I remembered
the LORD; and my prayer went up to You,
into Your holy temple. . . . " So the LORD spoke
to the fish, and it vomited Jonah onto dry land.*

JONAH 2:7, 10 NKJV

When we are in too deep, when there seems no way out of the trouble we've gotten ourselves into, we turn to the Lord. In that moment of distress and suffocating darkness, we confess how badly we messed up and thank Him for putting up with us. And in that moment, upon hearing that pain and remorse, God speaks to our giant fish and suddenly we are free, back in His light! How wonderful to be on God's dry land.

Simple

*But he's already made it plain how to live, what to do,
what GOD is looking for in men and women. It's quite simple:
Do what is fair and just to your neighbor, be compassionate
and loyal in your love, and don't take yourself
too seriously—take God seriously.*

MICAH 6:8 MSG

If we spent more time thinking about God than about ourselves, our past, and our future, we'd live a lot more fully in the present. After all, there's nothing we can do about the past. It can't be changed. And there's no point worrying about the future. It isn't here yet. Our time would be better spent living in the present with the Presence—and living it His way, with justice, love, compassion, and a good sense of humor.

No Matter What

*The Lord is good, a Strength and Stronghold in the day
of trouble; He knows (recognizes, has knowledge of,
and understands) those who take refuge and trust in Him.*

NAHUM 1:7 AMP

God knows exactly what we are all about. He totally sees us for who we truly are. And He still loves us. He still wants to and is ready to take care of us when we run into trouble. So, if things are looking bleak, a plan backfired and you're in a tough spot, don't despair. Don't be afraid to approach God, and run beneath His wing. He gets it. He gets you. And He's ready to take you in—no matter what.

CLIMBING HIGHER AND HIGHER

The Lord God is my Strength, my personal bravery, and my invincible army; He makes my feet like hinds' feet and will make me to walk [not to stand still in terror, but to walk] and make [spiritual] progress upon my high places.

HABAKKUK 3:19 AMP

What a wonderful life a Christian woman has. You have got God as your Strength, a veritable spiritual army that will come to your aid at any moment you need Him. Because of Him you are agile enough to walk where no woman has gone before. Because of Him, you don't fear anything. You will never be a deer caught in the headlights but one that continues to climb higher and higher, ever closer to God. That's something to celebrate!

OH, WHAT A SAVIOR!

"For the LORD your God is living among you.
He is a mighty savior. He will take delight in you with
gladness. With his love, he will calm all your fears.
He will rejoice over you with joyful songs."

ZEPHANIAH 3:17 NLT

What a way to start the day! Planting firmly into the soil of your mind, body, and soul that God is living among us. That the One who saved you, Jesus, delights in you. He's tickled pink that you are in His life! Wrapped in His arms, He gives you the peace only He can give. He is so happy with you that He can't help but burst out in song. He's more than a Savior—He's what you can't live without! So rejoice in the Lord today, and watch it spill over onto others. That Jesus joy—it's contagious!

ENERGY SOURCE

*" 'Get to work! For I am with you.' The GOD-of-the-Angel-
Armies is speaking! 'Put into action the word I covenanted
with you when you left Egypt. I'm living and breathing among
you right now. Don't be timid. Don't hold back.' "*
HAGGAI 2:4–5 MSG

God has given each woman a special role to play or job to do in her time here on earth. Whether she is a housewife, a career woman, single, married, a mother, an evangelist, a writer, or a preacher, God is walking beside her right now. He is the main source of her energy. With that thought in her mind, she need not be shy but boldly follow the course God has laid out for her. Holding nothing back, she reveals herself to be a woman of God's strength!

An Awesome Harvest

"I will save you, and you shall be a blessing.
Do not fear, let your hands be strong."

ZECHARIAH 8:13 NKJV

How awesome to think that God has made you a blessing. Because you are a boon to others, He doesn't want you to be afraid of anything. Instead, God wants you to look around you. Take in everything and everyone. Where, amid all the ups and downs of this world, can you be a blessing to someone else, with or without her knowledge? Whose day can you make today? Whether it be through making food, donating money, or helping to rebuild someone's home, step out into the world. Be God's blessing. Sow your love and compassion, and reap an awesome harvest.

A FLOOD OF BLESSINGS

❦

"Bring all the tithes into the storehouse so there will be enough food in my Temple. If you do," says the LORD of Heaven's Armies, "I will open the windows of heaven for you. I will pour out a blessing so great you won't have enough room to take it in! Try it! Put me to the test!"

MALACHI 3:10 NLT

Can you, daughter of God, imagine that just by giving God His due, He will more than double the investment of time and money you make to your church? And it won't just be a little drop of a return—but a flood of blessings that will come your way. Not sure it's true? Try it. It's God's promise. And you know He never lies! You can always count on Him—and His blessings.

COURAGEOUS

"She will bring forth a Son, and you shall call His name JESUS, for He will save His people from their sins." . . . "And they shall call His name Immanuel," which is translated, "God with us."

MATTHEW 1:21, 23 NKJV

Imagine an angel coming to your fiancé, telling him that you are going to have a son and name Him Jesus, but everybody will call Him Immanuel. Can you imagine being Mary, who had her own angel bearing news? What amazing revelations for a young couple just starting out! Fortunately for all of us, these two were no shirkers of duty. Joseph valiantly protected Mary, and Mary bravely bore the Savior into our world. Courage breeds courage. Ask God how you, too, can be brave for Jesus, who walks with you today.

TOUGH LOVE

"You have heard the law that says, 'Love your neighbor' and hate your enemy. But I say, love your enemies! Pray for those who persecute you!"

MATTHEW 5:43–44 NLT

When someone hurts us, it seems instinctual to hurt them right back. But Jesus would have us do just the opposite. Turning the other cheek seems especially tough for mothers, for nothing gets us more vengeful than someone who hurts our child—or any child for that matter. But what feels right instinctually is often not right spiritually. Shock your enemies by loving them. In doing so, you'll be imitating the God who loved us while *we* were still offenders. While you're at it, pray for your enemies. It may not change them for the better, but it will definitely change you.

Private Room

When you pray, go into your [most] private room, and, closing the door, pray to your Father, Who is in secret; and your Father, Who sees in secret, will reward you in the open.
MATTHEW 6:6 AMP

Sometimes it's hard for a busy woman to find any privacy, especially if she's got young kids. But how cool to know your "private room" for prayer doesn't have to be an actual room. It can be a mountaintop, desert, garden, or kitchen. Or it can be a place you envision in your mind while you sit in a pew, car, office, or train. What it's not to be is a platform where you impress other people with your overplayed oratory skills. It's simply a safe place where you go, within or without, and meet with God privately. That's a reward in itself.

FREE-FLUNG FORGIVENESS

"In prayer there is a connection between what God does and what you do. You can't get forgiveness from God, for instance, without also forgiving others. If you refuse to do your part, you cut yourself off from God's part."
MATTHEW 6:14–15 MSG

This thing about our forgiving others in order to be forgiven by God seems like a great challenge in this oftentimes dog-eat-dog society. But, as Christians, we are to travel a different road, one that seems illogical to the world around us. Because we are to love others as God loves us, we are also to forgive others, as God has forgiven us. When we do so, we break the chain of "getting even," find true freedom with others and especially with God, and can rechannel our vengeful energy into more constructive areas. So heal the hostility. Break free with forgiveness. Fling yourself into love.

Nothing Else Needed

"Where your treasure is,
there your heart will be also."
MATTHEW 6:21 NKJV

Every once in a while, when we see the perfect purse, the most darling pair of shoes, or an absolute must-buy outfit, we women can literally break out in a cold sweat. But, really, how many purses, pairs of shoes, or changes of clothing does one woman need? And how long will they stay in style? Rather than focusing all our attention on keeping one step ahead of the Joneses and spending all our money on the latest fashions, God would have us focus on Him and spend our love, compassion, charity, and forgiveness on others. The treasures on earth are passing fancies. But the treasures in heaven, on all of God and His good things, are where our hearts should be. For nothing else is needed.

THE POWER OF PERSISTENCE

"Keep on asking, and you will receive what you ask for. Keep on seeking, and you will find. Keep on knocking, and the door will be opened to you. For everyone who asks, receives. Everyone who seeks, finds. And to everyone who knocks, the door will be opened."
MATTHEW 7:7–8 NLT

Women have many dreams—having the perfect career, finding the right man, becoming a mother, holding that first grandchild, and more. But sometimes we either forget to ask God about these things or we give up if we don't get our prayers answered overnight. God loves the persistence of His people. And each time we go to Him, our prayers morph into the prayers He wants us to pray. So keep asking, keep seeking, keep knocking. Don't give up. Your answer may be just around the corner and through the next door.

DETERMINED FAITH

*She kept saying to herself, If I only touch His garment,
I shall be restored to health. Jesus turned around and, seeing
her, He said, Take courage, daughter! Your faith has made
you well. And at once the woman was restored to health.*

MATTHEW 9:21–22 AMP

Imagine bleeding for twelve years, then hearing about a man who could heal you. You get this thought stuck in your head: *If I just get close enough to touch Him, I will be made well.* It is this kind of faith that makes Jesus take notice. This woman with an issue of blood had no ifs, ands, or buts in her thoughts. She knew. She determined. She braved. And as a result she was made whole once more. May you approach Jesus with your own such assurance and hear Him say, "Daughter, your faith has made you well."

God's Greatest Treasure

Even the very hairs of your head are all numbered.
Fear not, then; you are of more value than many sparrows.

MATTHEW 10:30–31 AMP

Women love it when someone notices and compliments them on their hair. So just imagine how fabulous it is that God not only notices each one of your hairs but actually has them all counted! On top of that, He truly values you—and what you say, think, do, believe. He's paying attention to your every thought, word, and worry. Although it may seem like you are a tiny cog in a big wheel, take heart in the fact that God knows and loves every intimate detail about you. You are so precious in His sight; there's no need to be afraid. So go forward today with faith and courage, knowing you are one of His greatest treasures.

DIRECT CONNECTION

" 'I was hungry, and you fed me. I was thirsty, and you gave me a drink. I was a stranger, and you invited me into your home. I was naked, and you gave me clothing. I was sick, and you cared for me. I was in prison, and you visited me.' "

MATTHEW 25:35–36 NLT

It's true that today's woman is busy with family, work, school, home, and church and all the organizations that come with those responsibilities. Yet God would have us serve an even greater cause—reaching out a hand to the hungry, thirsty, stranger, naked, sick, and imprisoned. By doing so, we are connecting directly with Christ. For He can be found amid the overlooked, the ignored, the abused who need our love and assistance. Look around you today. Where can you find and serve Christ?

Becoming a Landscaper

*"I tell you the truth, you can say to this mountain,
'May you be lifted up and thrown into the sea,'
and it will happen. But you must really believe
it will happen and have no doubt in your heart."*

MARK 11:23 NLT

A woman often has a huge range of obstacles before her, so many that sometimes they can begin to weigh her down. Yet this is not so with a woman of faith, right? Jesus says straight-out that you have the power to move those mountainous obstacles. How? By truly believing that you can. That means not one iota of doubt can be in your heart. Still not so sure? Then ask God to increase your faith as you daily pray His mountain-moving promise. Before you know it, you'll find yourself a tried-and-true landscaper!

A Conduit of Love

*"The most important commandment is this: 'Listen, O Israel!
The LORD our God is the one and only LORD. And you must
love the LORD your God with all your heart, all your soul,
all your mind, and all your strength.' The second is equally
important: 'Love your neighbor as yourself.'"*

MARK 12:29–31 NLT

Jesus has whittled down all the commandments and regulations into two simple rules: love God with all of your being and love others as yourself. It sounds really easy. And it is! Until you get out of bed. Then all your good intentions sometimes just fly right out the window. So how is a woman to cope? Go to God! Ask Him to constantly and consistently flood you with His love, and allow His love to flow through you to others. Then rise to the challenge.

THE CHRIST CONNECTION

Jesus came down with them and took His stand on a level spot. . . . And all the multitude were seeking to touch Him, for healing power was all the while going forth from Him and curing them all [saving them from severe illnesses or calamities].

LUKE 6:17, 19 AMP

Jesus is standing before you. On level ground He has taken His place and is waiting. All He needs is for you to meet Him where He stands, to reach out to Him, wanting to touch Him. For He knows what you need. His power is emanating from Him, looking for a woman to heal, to soothe, to hold. Reach out today. Feel His power. Hear His voice. Make that Christ connection. And the kingdom of God is yours!

A NEEDED DEED

"What do you think? Which of the three became a neighbor to the man attacked by robbers?" "The one who treated him kindly," the religion scholar responded. Jesus said, "Go and do the same."

LUKE 10:36–37 MSG

After Jesus tells a scholar we are to love our neighbors as ourselves, the student asks for a definition of *neighbor*. Then Jesus goes on to tell the story of the Good Samaritan (see Luke 10:25–37). As it turns out, the neighbor is whoever we see that needs help. It can be the people next door to your house, your pew, or your desk. It can be the woman in the park, on the subway, or at the mall. Instead of focusing on your smart phone, focus on Christ's command. Look up and all around you for that neighbor in need, and do your good deed.

Such Love

"This is how much God loved the world: He gave his Son, his one and only Son. And this is why: so that no one need be destroyed; by believing in him, anyone can have a whole and lasting life."

JOHN 3:16 MSG

Imagine sacrificing your son, the one through whom your world was made, for the sake of others. Deserting Him at His greatest hour of need, just so that others could be saved. That's how much God loved the world. So that you would not be destroyed. How can you ever pay God back? By trusting in, clinging to Jesus. By making Him your all in all. By loving others as much as He loved you. By thanking Him for the gift of eternal life. By making each day count—for Him.

TWO LITTLE WORDS

Jesus wept.
JOHN 11:35 NKJV

Although this verse—"Jesus wept"—is short, it still packs a punch. These two little words speak of Jesus' great compassion for people. And although this phrase is somewhat sad, it lifts us up. For this reminds us that Jesus knows exactly what we're going through in every phase of our life. He knows the pain, the strain, the stress of living in this world. He also knows the joy, the beauty, the love that surrounds us. He knows what it means to have a bad day, to grieve for a loss, to be betrayed, to be treated harshly, to not fit the norm. Thus we are free to run to Him for any little thing. He's one man who will always listen. In fact, He is straining to hear from you. Talk to Him today. Tell Him all. He'll understand.

AWESOME POWER

Suddenly, there was a bright light in the cell,
and an angel of the Lord stood before Peter.
The angel struck him on the side to awaken him and said,
"Quick! Get up!" And the chains fell off his wrists.

ACTS 12:7 NLT

Prayer power is amazing! When fellow believers are praying with every part of their being, the world fills with light. Angels come to the rescue—even while we're sleeping! Our chains—of addiction, self-pity, unforgiveness, self-reliance, and so forth—just fall off. Next thing you know, we are walking, as if in a dream. We're outside. Free again! Once we come to our "senses," we realize the miracle of God's working in our life. So never give up! Do not surrender to doubt and fear. Keep on praying for yourself and others. Realize and prove the awesome power of prayer.

THE POWER OF PRAISE

But about midnight, as Paul and Silas were praying and singing hymns of praise to God, and the [other] prisoners were listening to them, suddenly there was a great earthquake.
ACTS 16:25–26 AMP

Prayer is a super weapon. But so is singing hymns of praise to God! After all, when Paul and Silas prayed and sang after being beaten, thrown into a dungeon, and chained to the wall, a great earthquake shook the prison, opened all the doors, and unchained everyone! So, when you feel beaten down by life, a prisoner of problems, and fettered to your worries, try praying, then singing a song of praise. Before you know it, you'll be free. That's the power of praise!

Eyes Up

Abraham was first named "father" and then became a father because he dared to trust God to do what only God could do: raise the dead to life, with a word make something out of nothing. When everything was hopeless, Abraham believed anyway, deciding to live not on the basis of what he saw he couldn't do but on what God said he would do.

Romans 4:17–18 MSG

How wonderful to believe something just because God said so. That's how Abraham realized the dream God had given him. He knew God—who created the entire world—could, with one word, "make something out of nothing." Are things looking hopeless to you? Believe anyway. Keep your eyes on what God can do, instead of what you can't do. Oh, daughter, dare to trust God! No matter what, believe Him. And all your dreams *will* come true! That's His promise!

HIGH EXPECTATIONS

This resurrection life you received from God is not a timid,
grave-tending life. It's adventurously expectant,
greeting God with a childlike "What's next, Papa?"
ROMANS 8:15 MSG

This new life in Christ is awesome! Now that we're on board with what God wants for our lives, that He is with us every step of the way, we can be bold! Adventurers! Instead of cowering in fear, we are wonderfully courageous women, knowing that nothing can hurt us on this side of eternal life. We await God's orders with high expectations, and He leads us to more than we can imagine. One step at a time He takes us closer and closer to the prize set before us, as we, His daughters, continually ask, "Where to now, Abba?"

THE INTERPRETER

We don't know what God wants us to pray for. But the
Holy Spirit prays for us with groanings that cannot be
expressed in words. And the Father who knows all hearts
knows what the Spirit is saying, for the Spirit pleads
for us believers in harmony with God's own will.

ROMANS 8:26–27 NLT

Our mother is ill, and we've become stressed-out caretakers. Our daughter is rebelling, and we don't know how to reach her. Our marriage is teetering, and we're not sure how to save it. Sometimes, we hardly know how to pray. But we feel an intense desire to lay our lives out before God, begging for His help. Fortunately, we have the Holy Spirit to interpret our groans, our sighs, our cries to God. So go to prayer, knowing that God will hear your heart and respond with exactly what you need.

ACCORDING TO PLAN

*We are assured and know that [God being a partner
in their labor] all things work together and are
[fitting into a plan] for good to and for those who love God
and are called according to [His] design and purpose.*

ROMANS 8:28 AMP

What a relief knowing that what sometimes seems like a mishmash of life is actually somehow all coming together. That all the decisions we've made, everything that's happened need not be analyzed but seen as something God actually had planned for us. And that everything about this plan has not only made us what we are today but also worked well together for God's purpose. So no need looking back, really. And no need to worry about the future. Whatever is going to happen—be it good or bad—is all in God's hands. And that's the best place our lives can be.

ORIGINAL DESIGN

Give your bodies to God because of all he has done for you. . . .
This is truly the way to worship him. Don't copy the
behavior and customs of this world, but let God transform
you into a new person by changing the way you think.
Then you will learn to know God's will for you.

ROMANS 12:1–2 NLT

It's so easy to get caught up in this world's passions and pleasures. Each day we're inundated by the media, being told we need this or should want that. Yet, as Christians, we are to imitate Christ, not the latest fashion model, starlet, or American idol. When you accepted Christ, you began changing into who God originally designed you to be. So don't stop now. Give yourself up to Him—and only Him—each day. Let Him continue to transform you at the core into the apple of His eye.

A Way Out

The temptations in your life are no different from what others experience. And God is faithful. He will not allow the temptation to be more than you can stand. When you are tempted, he will show you a way out so that you can endure.

1 Corinthians 10:13 NLT

Women often face a myriad of temptations, whether we're being enticed to buy an item we really can't afford, eat a second bowl of ice cream, or scarf down a chocolate Easter bunny originally bought for the kids. In each of those circumstances, God shows us a way out, an escape route. Our job is to actually look for the Exit sign. So before buying that new dress or adding another inch to your hips, take a deep breath and look for God. He's waving you toward the exit ramp.

FOREVER LOVE

*Faith, hope, love abide [faith—conviction and belief
respecting man's relation to God and divine things;
hope—joyful and confident expectation of eternal salvation;
love—true affection for God and man, growing out of God's
love for and in us], these three; but the greatest of these is love.*

1 CORINTHIANS 13:13 AMP

Most women are drawn to romantic movies. There is something so special and heartwarming about a man and a woman falling in love. It piques our interest because we, too, love being in love. The love we have for our man is special, but the love we have for and from God is even more amazing. In fact, it's the greatest thing that exists on heaven and earth. Yes, faith and hope will one day be realized by us in heaven, but God's love will endure forever and ever.

E FOR EFFORT

❧◦◦◦ ◦◦◦❧

Be firm (steadfast), immovable, always abounding in
the work of the Lord [always being superior, excelling,
doing more than enough in the service of the Lord],
knowing and being continually aware that your labor in
the Lord is not futile [it is never wasted or to no purpose].

I CORINTHIANS 15:58 AMP

Some Sundays when we show up to teach adult Sunday school, our classroom is empty. Turns out everyone went to the firehouse breakfast. Other days we come with all our craft supplies for kids' church, and all the children are home with the flu. When these things happen, we may feel as if our effort has been wasted. But anything and everything we do for the Lord has a purpose. So keep up the good work, ladies. God sees what you're doing and is finding a way to use it for His good.

CHAIN OF COMFORT

God is our merciful Father and the source of all comfort.
He comforts us in all our troubles so that we can comfort
others. When they are troubled, we will be able to
give them the same comfort God has given us.

2 CORINTHIANS 1:3–4 NLT

When we suffer the death of a loved one, we almost feel as if we will never see daylight again. But then someone comes along, another woman who has suffered the same loss. She needn't say anything. Her very presence gives us peace, for we know she knows what we feel. It's a chain of comfort: from God, to another, to us. When the darkness abates, when we heal once more, we see another woman bowed down with grief. We approach and the chain continues. What a comfort. What a woman. What a God. What links of love.

EYES OF FAITH

We walk by faith [we regulate our lives and conduct ourselves by our conviction or belief respecting man's relationship to God and divine things, with trust and holy fervor; thus we walk] not by sight or appearance.

2 CORINTHIANS 5:7 AMP

There are those who believe we are born, live, die, and that's it. Once the physical world is gone, there is only emptiness. Yet those of us who believe in things that we cannot see—God the Father, Jesus the Son, and the Holy Spirit—know there is so much more. This is what gives us hope. After all, gravity exists and cannot be seen. The same can be said of love, which is not only invisible but also eternal. Ladies, keep your eyes of faith on the divine and you will never, ever walk or live alone—on earth or in heaven.

Major Do-Over

This means that anyone who belongs to Christ has become a new person. The old life is gone; a new life has begun!

2 CORINTHIANS 5:17 NLT

Life doesn't offer us many do-overs. Yet all who believe in Christ get a major one—an entire life do-over! When we begin to believe, when we get serious about our faith, when we graft ourselves onto the Christ tree, an amazing transformation occurs. We become brand-new. We become empowered by the greatest force on heaven and earth—love! Every step we take is on the new road to freedom in Christ, the One who forever changed the world. We go from caterpillar to butterfly, never to crawl again. Instead, we take flight, soar between heaven and earth, forever transformed.

MINDING MENTAL MEANDERINGS

We lead every thought and purpose away captive into the obedience of Christ (the Messiah, the Anointed One).
2 CORINTHIANS 10:5 AMP

Thoughts can be wild things. From concerns about children, to worries about job loss, to fears about finances, your mental meanderings can really bring you down. They can keep you from seeing with the eyes of faith. So blinded, you may find yourself groping your way through life—afraid, suspicious, worried, haunted, trapped. So don't let your thoughts run wild. Pay attention to what you are saying to yourself. Ever alert, endeavor to replace negative thoughts with uplifting, God-healing scripture. For memorizing Bible verses will do a woman's mind—and body—nothing but good. And 2 Corinthians 10:5, the verse above, is a great place to start as you begin minding your mental meanderings.

Ever-Expanding Return

Let's not allow ourselves to get fatigued doing good.
At the right time we will harvest a good crop if we don't
give up, or quit. Right now, therefore, every time we
get the chance, let us work for the benefit of all, starting
with the people closest to us in the community of faith.

Galatians 6:9 MSG

With so many opportunities to do good in this world, women, natural-born nurturers, may feel as if it's a losing battle. How will we ever accomplish all that needs to be done? Well, we needn't worry. If we all just keep helping, beginning with those at home and at church, we'll eventually reap a good harvest. So simply keep nurturing where you naturally can, confident that everything will come out right for you and the lives of those you touch, remembering that tender loving care tends to yield an ever-expanding return.

MASTER'S PLAN

We are God's [own] handiwork (His workmanship),
recreated in Christ Jesus, [born anew] that we may do those
good works which God predestined (planned beforehand)
for us [taking paths which He prepared ahead of time],
that we should walk in them [living the good life which
He prearranged and made ready for us to live].

EPHESIANS 2:10 AMP

Women love to have a plan. It makes us feel secure, almost as if we are in control. So how great is it that when we are born again in Christ, we are able to begin doing the things God planned way back. We begin walking on paths He's already laid out for us. We begin having the life He wanted us to have. That Master's plan—a relief and an adventure at the same time! Walk on, ladies! Walk on!

Empowered by God

I pray that from his glorious, unlimited resources he will empower you with inner strength through his Spirit. . . . Now all glory to God, who is able, through his mighty power at work within us, to accomplish infinitely more than we might ask or think.
EPHESIANS 3:16, 20 NLT

When we bow down to Christ, laying aside our weakness, we rise in His power within, stronger than we ever have been before. Through us, God works miracles. We suddenly find ourselves accomplishing something we never thought possible. Something beyond our imagination and understanding. Secure in His love, dreams begin coming true. It's time to stretch, ladies. Reach high! And witness the miracle of God's power within taking form without.

GOOD MORNING, GOD!

*Be constantly renewed in the spirit of your mind [having a
fresh mental and spiritual attitude], and put on the new
nature (the regenerate self) created in God's image.*
EPHESIANS 4:23–24 AMP

Each new day gives us a chance to make a fresh start, spiritually and mentally. And a great way to start that new day is by greeting God with a smile, a praise, and a prayer. Try this: Each morning, jump out of bed, and say, "*Good* morning, God!" Then greet Jesus and the Holy Spirit the same way. Acknowledge aloud that you know they will be with you, helping you to do all you have been called that day to do. Thank God for all your blessings—past, present, and future. Set out knowing that the three-in-one God is *with* you and going to do amazing things *through* you.

SHARPEST TOOLS

Take the sword of the Spirit, which is the word of God. Pray in the Spirit at all times and on every occasion. Stay alert and be persistent in your prayers for all believers everywhere.

EPHESIANS 6:17–18 NLT

The sharpest tools in our spiritual shed are God's Word and our prayers. When we wield them, nothing can defeat us. When we use them, no weed can choke out our good intentions. To keep God's Word sharp, we need to study it, memorize it, believe it, and apply it to our lives. To keep our prayers on point, we need to speak to God daily and have a praise-filled attitude from sunup to sundown. In a constant state of prayer and praise, with God's Word recited back to Him, nothing can defeat His women, armed with the sharpest tools in God's shed.

The Heart of the Matter

I pray that your love will overflow more and more, and that
you will keep on growing in knowledge and understanding.
For I want you to understand what really matters.

PHILIPPIANS 1:9–10 NLT

It's amazing how one kind word can totally lift the spirit, how a simple smile can change a person's day, how five minutes of considerate and thoughtful listening can relieve another's burden. The more you learn about and understand God, the more you realize what is really important—you loving God and others. As you spend time in His presence, He fills you with His eternal love, which cannot help but spill over onto others. Your job, let it flow out and touch someone. Whom can you encourage with a kind word? To whom can you lift a simple smile? For whom can you lend a listening ear? Go forward in love today.

A Woman Empowered

❦

[For my determined purpose is] that I may know Him [that I may progressively become more deeply and intimately acquainted with Him, perceiving and recognizing and understanding the wonders of His Person more strongly and more clearly], and that I may in that same way come to know the power outflowing from His resurrection [which it exerts over believers].

PHILIPPIANS 3:10 AMP

Wow! Resurrection power. The love Jesus poured out for us on the cross, the love that raised Him from the dead for our sakes, that's some pretty strong stuff. And it's available to you each and every moment of every day. If you make it your aim and purpose to fully believe in Jesus, to study Him, to walk in His steps His way, you, too, will know His amazing strength. You will be a woman empowered by God, a woman to be reckoned with.

WISE AHEAD

❧⟡❧

*I press on to possess that perfection for which Christ
Jesus first possessed me. No, dear brothers and sisters,
I have not achieved it, but I focus on this one thing:
Forgetting the past and looking forward to what lies ahead.*

PHILIPPIANS 3:12–13 NLT

Ah, forgetting the past. If only. But, yet, it's obviously possible. The apostle Paul did it. So can you! And although it may be something you have to do every day, that's okay, too! When something you regret or cannot forgive enters your mind, tell it to take off, go away. You aren't going to waste your energy on what you can't change. You're wiser than that. Instead of mooning over the could've-should've-would'ves, you're going to use all your power to go forward. Good move!

No Better Way

Rejoice in the Lord always.
I will say it again: Rejoice!
PHILIPPIANS 4:4 NIV

Yesterday may not have gone as well as you'd hoped it would. And today looks like it's shaping up to be another tough one. Energy is lagging. Hope isn't where it usually is. Everything just seems a little off. But wait. There's something you can do to change all of this up: Rejoice in the Lord! Sing a song of praise. Get out that old hymnal, or grab the iPod and cue up some great contemporary Christian music. Start dancing with the Lord. Take joy in each and every move you make. He is with you! He is your very own! He loves you with all of His heart! He sees you as the apple of His eye! Rejoice in the Lord! Yes, rejoice! There's no better way to live!

A TRUE LADY

Let your gentleness be evident to all.
The Lord is near.
PHILIPPIANS 4:5 NIV

The word *gentlewoman* is hardly used at all anymore. Yet being called such is a wonderful compliment to any woman. It implies that you come from a good family and have good breeding. That you are a true *lady* in every sense of the word. But of *course* you come from a good family—you are God's daughter, the daughter of a King! A royal princess. There is no longer any need to be power hungry, to claw your way to the top—you are already there. You are indeed a gentlewoman—loving, kind, soft spoken, selfless, Word-wise, comforting. And the best thing about it is that those who see the *gentle* woman so obvious in you, know that God isn't very far behind.

CALM IN CHRIST

Don't worry about anything; instead, pray about everything.
Tell God what you need, and thank him for all he has done.
Then you will experience God's peace, which exceeds
anything we can understand. His peace will guard your
hearts and minds as you live in Christ Jesus.
PHILIPPIANS 4:6–7 NLT

Got some things on your mind? Are they making your brow furrow, your stomach clench? If so, take them to God. Tell Him *everything*—and be specific! Don't leave anything out. Tell Him all your intentions, and ask Him to align them to His will. Most of all, praise Him for yesterday's blessings, those awaiting you today, and those in the future. Afterward, allow God to fill you with His peace. You'll be amazed at how relaxed you are, your heart and mind calm in Christ instead of churning in chaos.

Mind Fill

You'll do best by filling your minds and meditating on things true, noble, reputable, authentic, compelling, gracious—the best, not the worst; the beautiful, not the ugly; things to praise, not things to curse.

PHILIPPIANS 4:8 MSG

Today's TV shows, computer games, movies, newspapers, and books all seem to have dark, dreary, menacing themes. It's enough to send even the most upbeat person into the lowest of funks. And when we are low, we have less energy to do God's work. What's the answer? Feed your mind on good things. Watch a Hallmark instead of a horror movie, read inspirational instead of murder-filled books. Praise instead of pout. Consistently stop and check your thoughts. If they're dark, throw some godly light on them. Make a list of your blessings and successes each and every day. Go for the positive—and that's what you'll get.

Making Do

I have learned how to be content with whatever I have. . . . And this same God who takes care of me will supply all your needs from his glorious riches, which have been given to us in Christ Jesus.
Philippians 4:11, 19 nlt

Looking back over your life, chances are you were happiest during those times you had to "make do." You were filled with the joy of finding a dress for half off, getting a good deal on a child's desk at a thrift shop, or telling stories on Friday night instead of going to the movies. Each event was special in its own way because you were content with doing what you could with what you had. Know that the same God who gives you that wonder-filled sense of contentment will always supply you with all you really need—which, thank God, is more than enough!

SUPER-SPIRITUAL STRENGTH

I have strength for all things in Christ Who empowers me
[I am ready for anything and equal to anything
through Him Who infuses inner strength into me;
I am self-sufficient in Christ's sufficiency].

PHILIPPIANS 4:13 AMP

Ever hear of women performing amazing physical feats of strength in order to save a loved one? There are reported cases of a mother lifting a car to save her son and a daughter upending a car to save her dad. One woman fought off two bears to save her children, and two teenage sisters lifted a tractor to save their father! Amazing, right? Yet even more amazing is the super-*spiritual* strength you have in Christ. You are infused with it! It's coursing through your inner woman right now! No need to fear or fret about anything—Christ has powered you up to face everything! What a lift!

In Light and Love

God rescued us from dead-end alleys and dark dungeons.
He's set us up in the kingdom of the Son he loves so much,
the Son who got us out of the pit we were in, got rid
of the sins we were doomed to keep repeating.

COLOSSIANS 1:13–14 MSG

Before coming to Christ, you may have been in some really dark places—spiritually and physically. But God has rescued you from those shadows. He has brought you into the light and love of His Son. You have been brought up and out of the abyss. You no longer do things that once made you disappointed in yourself. Each and every day you grow stronger, freer, happier. You are a princess now. Praise God, the King. Praise Christ, the Savior and Son. Go forward in the truth and power of His light and love.

FROM THE BEGINNING

Everything, absolutely everything, above and below, visible and invisible, rank after rank after rank of angels— everything got started in him and finds its purpose in him. He was there before any of it came into existence and holds it all together right up to this moment.

COLOSSIANS 1:15–16 MSG

Jesus was not only God made visible on earth. He was also the beginning of everything that we see—and all that we don't see! And it is in this amazing master crafts-man, the Word come to life, that we find our true pur-pose—to love God, ourselves, and each other. And it is in this Son of God, who suffered and died for us, that everything in this world is *still* being held together. What power! What love! What a magnificent Savior! Praise Him today for all that—and more—from beginning to end!

Spiritual Outlook

Since you have been raised to new life with Christ,
set your sights on the realities of heaven, where
Christ sits in the place of honor at God's right hand.
Think about the things of heaven, not the things of earth.

Colossians 3:1–2 nlt

When you walk with your eyes focused on the ground before you, chances are you'll miss many things that are going on *around* you. But God wants your eyes on things above, focused on Him. He wants your eyes up, not down. Your thoughts on Him, not things of this earth. When you look at things from His heavenly point of view, your outlook on everything changes and, in turn, so do you. With this new vantage point, you see the true reality of this world. So, chin up, ladies. God's just waiting to catch your eye—and mind!

THE NEW YOU

[You] have clothed yourselves with the new [spiritual self], which is [ever in the process of being] renewed and remolded into [fuller and more perfect knowledge upon] knowledge after the image (the likeness) of Him Who created it.

COLOSSIANS 3:10 AMP

The "new you" is looking pretty good. Each day you are being renewed within and without. You are getting closer and closer to bearing the image of Jesus. Your nature is gentler, kinder, wiser than it once was. You are more giving, patient, loving than before. Chances are you aren't perfect. But you are coming along nicely. Never beat yourself up because you're not where you yet want to be. Instead, praise God because of how far He has already brought you. Every day is a new day and a time to celebrate the new you.

GODLY AMBITION

Make it your goal to live a quiet life, minding your own business and working with your hands, just as we instructed you before. Then people who are not Christians will respect the way you live, and you will not need to depend on others.

1 THESSALONIANS 4:11–12 NLT

L et's face it. People are watching you. Nonbelievers want to know if you have really been changed by Jesus, if you walk the talk. So are you keeping calm in all circumstances, or are you panicking every time the stock market takes a dive? Are you keeping your nose out of the business of others, or are you the neighborhood gossip? Are you doing something productive, or are you simply idling? Remember: You may be the only Bible other people ever read.

To-Dos

Always try to do good to each other and to all people. Always be joyful. Never stop praying. Be thankful in all circumstances, for this is God's will for you who belong to Christ Jesus.

1 THESSALONIANS 5:15–18 NLT

I f everyone followed the guidelines presented in the above verses, this world would be a much better place. So why not try to follow these edicts, one day at a time? If you make that your intention at the beginning of each day, chances are you *will* change your part of the world, as well as change yourself. That's because all of these qualities you would work to imbue are those of Jesus. He was goodness and joy personified. He had a constant inner, and sometimes outer, dialogue with His Father. And when He thanked God, abundance followed. Yes, these verses would make a great "what would Jesus to-do" list.

HE WILL DO IT

Faithful is He Who is calling you [to Himself]
and utterly trustworthy, and He will also do it
[fulfill His call by hallowing and keeping you].
1 THESSALONIANS 5:24 AMP

Whatever task God gives you to do, He will give you the strength to do it. Whatever dream He plants in your heart, He will give you the means to realize it. Whatever promises He makes, He will come through on. To do otherwise would go against His nature. For He never lies. And the word He gives never comes back void. So have faith, woman, that you already have the ability to do what God has created you to do. Step out in confidence. And all dreams—those of yours and God's—will come true.

HEARTFELT PEACE

Do not become weary or lose heart in doing right
[but continue in well-doing without weakening]. . . .
Now may the Lord of peace Himself grant you His peace
(the peace of His kingdom) at all times and in all ways
[under all circumstances and conditions, whatever comes].
2 THESSALONIANS 3:13, 16 AMP

Sometimes you may feel as if your godly efforts are getting you nowhere. For it seems as if wars are a perpetual evil, as well as bombings, shootings, kidnappings, molestations. . . The list goes on and on. But no matter how bad things seem, know that God is counting on women of the Way to keep on keeping on. To continue doing their part in His kingdom. And that's all you really need to know. So, peace within and without, sister. Stay strong in love and the Lord.

YOUR SPECIAL GIFT

*Do not neglect the gift which is in you,
[that special inward endowment] which was
directly imparted to you [by the Holy Spirit].*
1 TIMOTHY 4:14 AMP

Lady, you are special. God has made you that way. Within you is a gift no one else has. Have you discovered it yet? If so, are you using it to bring others to God, to somehow awaken them to His presence? For that's what your gift is there for. If you haven't yet discovered your unique gift—which may be singing, teaching, preaching, writing, painting, and so forth—spend some time in prayer. Ask God to reveal your special talent to you. Don't wait another day. Who knows but that you and your gift have come for such a time as this—and there's not a moment to lose!

THE RIGHT PATH

*Lust for money brings trouble and nothing but trouble.
Going down that path, some lose their footing in the
faith completely and live to regret it bitterly ever after.*

1 TIMOTHY 6:10 MSG

Most people seem to know that they can't take anything with them when they leave this world. Yet it doesn't stop the majority of the population from worshipping the almighty dollar. Although money has its place—to keep us sheltered, warm, dry, clothed, and fed—it should in no way take the place of God. Unfortunately, some people learn that lesson the hard way. Save yourself the pain. Keep money off the altar of your heart. Stand strong in your faith. Keep God on His throne, and you won't be thrown off the right path.

THREE SPIRITS

For God did not give us a spirit of timidity (of cowardice, of craven and cringing and fawning fear), but [He has given us a spirit] of power and of love and of calm and well-balanced mind and discipline and self-control.

2 TIMOTHY 1:7 AMP

In this world there are plenty of things to be afraid of—spiders, snakes, bats, dark alleys, violent storms—just to name a few. But thank God that He has equipped us with three other spirits—those of power, love, and self-control. That's an extremely effective arsenal. With these spirits in your pocket and your eyes on Christ, all worry, doubt, and fear dissipate. Next thing you know, you're walking on the very waters that caused you concern just moments before. And Christ is right there with you.

YOUR ROAD MAP

All Scripture is inspired by God and is useful to teach us what is true and to make us realize what is wrong in our lives. It corrects us when we are wrong and teaches us to do what is right.

2 TIMOTHY 3:16 NLT

The Bible—what a font of wisdom and instruction. The Old Testament stories are filled with life lessons of fellow flawed beings and believers of God. The Psalms contain songs that speak to human hearts, giving voice to sorrows and joys, fears and courage, frustration and success. The Proverbs overflow with practical wisdom. And the New Testament shows believers how to be like Christ. All that God has written is meant to help you find your way. It's your road map to heaven on earth. No GPS needed. Simply unfold the Word and allow it to enfold you.

GOOD ATTITUDE

Everything is pure to those whose hearts are pure. But nothing is pure to those who are corrupt and unbelieving, because their minds and consciences are corrupted. Such people claim they know God, but they deny him by the way they live.

TITUS 1:15–16 NLT

Nonbelievers seem to have a negative attitude about lots of things. They sometimes claim a belief in God when they're in trouble but then quickly deny, ignore, or insult Him when things are going well. Those whose hearts have been tainted see trouble everywhere. But believers in Christ, because they are filled with God's Word, have purer minds and consciences. Everything they see, as God said in the beginning, is "good." And with this attitude, their thoughts rise higher and higher. So stay lifted and pure in heart and mind. Live in the Word—night and day. Witness the Light.

INSIDE OUT

I didn't want to do anything without your consent.
I wanted you to help because you were willing,
not because you were forced.

PHILEMON 1:14 NLT

God never really forces anything. If we are to believe Him, we are to do so willingly, not because He insists upon it. It's all about free will. We are free to believe or disbelieve. We are free to do good or not do good. Everything must come from our heart. That's what makes God so easy to love. If you are serving God in a way that's not from your heart, maybe it's time to step back and see where you might serve Him more compassionately. For when you mix your willing service with love, as Jesus did, amazing things begin to happen—from the inside out!

He Knows, So Go

This High Priest of ours understands our weaknesses,
for he faced all of the same testings we do, yet he did not sin.
So let us come boldly to the throne of our gracious God.
There we will receive his mercy, and we will find
grace to help us when we need it most.

HEBREWS 4:15–16 NLT

How awesome to have Jesus, a High Priest who knows *exactly* what we're going through. He's actually walked this earth, breathed the same air we breathe. He knew grief at the death of a friend. He experienced abandonment by His followers and His Father. He knew the physical pain and emotional humiliation of a beating. He knew what it was like to be hated, spied on, and betrayed. Jesus is almost too familiar with what you are going through. So go to Him. He understands and is more than ready to help.

No Doubt

Now faith is the assurance of things hoped for,
the conviction of things not seen.
HEBREWS 11:1 NASB

This verse is so short yet so powerful. It's part of an introduction to a list of heroes of our faith, only two of whose names are women. The first, Sarah, believed that God would make her a mother even though she was well past childbearing age. God promised; she believed. The second, the harlot Rahab, having heard about all the God of Israel had done, welcomed Joshua's spies. Because she believed their God was the one true God, capable of doing anything and everything, she was saved when the walls of Jericho fell—*and* she became an ancestress of Jesus! What a testimony of faith for women today. Go forward, believing, as Sarah and Rahab did. No longer doubt the impossible, but be assured your hopes will one day become your reality!

FAITHFUL FOLLOWER

Without faith it is impossible to please and be satisfactory to Him. For whoever would come near to God must [necessarily] believe that God exists and that He is the rewarder of those who earnestly and diligently seek Him [out].

HEBREWS 11:6 AMP

Are you constantly looking over your shoulder, trying to figure out if you're on the right path? Do you get easily distracted, and forget to watch out to see where God may be leading you? Are you continually second-guessing His plans for your life? If so, God may be getting tired of you dragging your feet. Want to get somewhere great? Want to really please God? Gird up your faith. Believe that God is with you and leading you! Look for Him everywhere! Know that He has a great plan for your life—and that your only job is to be a willing, diligent, faithful follower.

A FAMILIAR GUIDE

[Urged on] by faith Abraham, when he was called, obeyed and went forth to a place which he was destined to receive as an inheritance; and he went, although he did not know or trouble his mind about where he was to go.

HEBREWS 11:8 AMP

Like He had for Abraham, God has a destination for you, a place He's leading you to. But you can forget about the earthly road map. Don't even begin charging your GPS. Just follow God and He'll lead you to where you are meant to be. Like Abraham, may you be so obedient that you don't even bother thinking about where you're headed. May your faith be as solid as Abraham's, who, although he was unfamiliar with the landscape, was *totally* familiar with his Guide. So don't worry. Just go. Just believe. God will get you to where you are meant to be!

HOLD ON!

Be satisfied with your present [circumstances and with what you have]; for He [God] Himself has said, I will not in any way fail you nor give you up nor leave you without support. [I will] not, [I will] not, [I will] not in any degree leave you helpless nor forsake nor let [you] down (relax My hold on you)! [Assuredly not!]

HEBREWS 13:5 AMP

The Amplified Bible really does this verse up. In interpreting the original language this verse was written in, you really get the point that God is definitely always going to be there for you. There is no way He's going anywhere without you. He's got you in His hand and will never, ever release His grip on you. So don't worry about whatever may be going on in your life. It's temporary. He's leading you to better days ahead. So just hold on!

LASTING REFUGE

*So we take comfort and are encouraged and confidently
and boldly say, The Lord is my Helper; I will not be
seized with alarm [I will not fear or dread or be terrified].
What can man do to me?*

HEBREWS 13:6 AMP

Getting stressed out? Wondering where the next dollar is going to come from or where the next madman with a gun or a bomb will strike? How about this violent weather? Are you safe anywhere these days? Yep! There's one place of refuge left—God. In Him, there is no need to be panicked about anything. Nothing here on earth can touch your soul or spirit. No one can tear you from God's hands. So get confident. Get bold. Don't worry. You're in the right place—God's arms.

GOD'S COURSE

If you need wisdom, ask our generous God, and he will give it to you. . . . But when you ask him, be sure that your faith is in God alone. Do not waver, for a person with divided loyalty is as unsettled as a wave of the sea that is blown and tossed by the wind. Such people should not expect to receive anything from the Lord.

JAMES 1:5–7 NLT

Everyone needs wisdom at some time or another. And how great that you can go to God and ask Him for it. The only thing is, you must be confident that He will give you the answer you need. Once you get on God's course, there's to be no going back, no taking another route later due to uncertainty. Instead, be steady. Full steam ahead. And God will get you where you need to go.

TRUE MOTIVES

You don't have what you want because you don't ask God for it. And even when you ask, you don't get it because your motives are all wrong—you want only what will give you pleasure.

JAMES 4:2–3 NLT

God, the ultimate Provider, is ready to give you whatever you want. Your only job is to ask Him for it. Like a child going to a parent, you are to go to God and lay your desire before Him. If you are asking with pure motives, you are sure to have your request granted. If you are asking for something with the wrong motives, He'll probably say no. So before asking God for anything, look deep within and determine your true motives. And know that whatever His answer is, He's doing what's best for you. That's what makes Him such a great Father! His motive is true love.

PRAYER POWER

The earnest (heartfelt, continued) prayer
of a righteous man makes tremendous
power available [dynamic in its working].
JAMES 5:16 AMP

When you are praying with your entire mind, soul, and spirit, when you are wholeheartedly coming before God, the heavens move. That's how much power prayer has! Imagine Elijah. He, too, was a mere mortal. Because of his heartfelt prayer, there was no rain for three and a half years. Then he prayed again, and it poured. (See James 5:17–18.) So, know, believe, have faith that there is power in folded hands. Go deep with each prayer. Focus all your attention on God, His Word, His power, and your request. Let your words and thoughts unfold before your almighty God. Move mountains with your faith.

FAITH LIFTS

*Don't be concerned about the outward beauty of fancy
hairstyles, expensive jewelry, or beautiful clothes.
You should clothe yourselves instead with the beauty
that comes from within, the unfading beauty of a gentle
and quiet spirit, which is so precious to God.*

1 PETER 3:3–4 NLT

When your inner beauty is shining forth, amazing things happen. Husbands disinterested in the whole "God thing" see something special in you and begin to thirst for a Savior. You become content with who you are. Worries cease. Your God-given gifts become evident and plentiful, bearing more and more fruit every day. Thus, you become more of service to others. Your love for one and all becomes even more obvious. And, with God's help, you become a woman after His own heart. All from cultivating the beauty within! That's one awesome faith lift!

ALL READY

*God has given us everything we need for living a godly
life. . . . Because of [Christ's] glory and excellence,
he has given us great and precious promises. These are
the promises that enable you to share his divine nature
and escape the world's corruption caused by human desires.*

2 PETER 1:3–4 NLT

How cool that you are already equipped to become
like Jesus. He has given you everything you need to
be selfless, loving, compassionate, peaceful, faithful, wise,
caring, patient, humble, and more! Because of all His
promises, valued beyond compare, there is nothing stop-
ping you from walking, talking, and living as Jesus did.
The more you get to know Him through the Word and
through prayer, the more like Him you will become. And
that's a good thing!

REAL LOVE

Let's not just talk about love; let's practice real love. This is the only way we'll know we're living truly, living in God's reality. It's also the way to shut down debilitating self-criticism. . . . For God is greater than our worried hearts and knows more about us than we do ourselves.

1 JOHN 3:18–20 MSG

God *is* love. And love is the most powerful force on heaven and earth. It's greater than faith and hope. But it's not something just to be gabbing about. It's something to put out there each and every day, especially if you are a mother, wife, and friend. And it's not just about loving others. God wants you to love yourself, as well. So stop that negative self-talk. See yourself for the precious princess you are in God's eyes. He knows more about you than you do. And He adores you.

ACCORD

This is not a new commandment but simply a repetition of our original and basic charter: that we love each other. Love means following his commandments, and his unifying commandment is that you conduct your lives in love. This is the first thing you heard, and nothing has changed.

2 JOHN 1:5–6 MSG

Love is not just a mandate for outside the assembly of believers. The people in every Christian church are to love one another, too. That means working together for the good of all. That means not holding grudges but putting others before you. That means not letting differences divide you. Instead, allow love, God's love, to unite you. Sing to the Lord a new song in accord, not discord. As much as you are able, live in love and peace with all. And God will smile on you and your church family.

GOOD EXAMPLES

Dear friend, don't let this bad example influence you.
Follow only what is good. Remember that those who do
good prove that they are God's children, and those
who do evil prove that they do not know God.

3 JOHN 1:11 NLT

Even in the church, you may come across someone who rebels against the leadership, makes terrible accusations against others, and basically causes division. Such a person is setting a bad example—inside and outside of the church. If you are ever in doubt of whose example to follow, look to Jesus. He is our best example of how to live a godly life. Follow in His footsteps and you will never go down the wrong path. And, in so doing, you will become a good example for others to follow.

TODAY'S BOOSTER

You, dear friends, must build each other up in your most holy faith, pray in the power of the Holy Spirit, and await the mercy of our Lord Jesus Christ, who will bring you eternal life. In this way, you will keep yourselves safe in God's love.

JUDE 1:20–21 NLT

God loves those who encourage others, building people up instead of tearing them down. One way to encourage people is by the things you say. Another way is giving your support, whether it be your money or helping hands. You can also encourage someone by lifting her up in prayer. In all these ways you honor not only yourself and others but also God and His love. So, who can you encourage? Who needs your prayers? Who is desperate for godly love? Give them a boost today.

THE OTHER SIDE

Behold, I stand at the door and knock; if anyone hears and listens to and heeds My voice and opens the door, I will come in to him and will eat with him, and he [will eat] with Me.

REVELATION 3:20 AMP

Jesus is standing just outside, on the other side of the door. It's up to you to open it. Are you listening for His knock? If you are, and you open the door, He's going to come right in. He's ready to sit down with you, to talk things over, to clue you in, to break bread with you. How cool is that? So keep your ears open. Listen for Jesus' footsteps. When He knocks, let Him in. Let Him reveal His thoughts to you. It will be a dinner conversation you'll remember forever.

Complete Joy

*God will wipe away every tear from their eyes; and death
shall be no more, neither shall there be anguish (sorrow and
mourning) nor grief nor pain any more, for the old conditions
and the former order of things have passed away.*

REVELATION 21:4 AMP

Imagine how wonderful it will be when there are no
more tears. When there is no more pain and grief.
When everything is totally new. It may be hard to visualize, but it will happen. And, as a faithful believer, one
day you will be there. Until then, live with this vision, this
hope as you travel through life. Love everyone you meet.
Pray and praise continually. Know that every trial, temptation, and tear is temporary. All of those things will one
day pass. And on that day, you will see Jesus in all His
glory. And in that moment, your joy will be complete.

Scripture Index